$\dfrac{120}{10} = 12 \quad \dfrac{\ }{15} = 8$

MARQUEE MINISTRY

✳ p. 26f DIALOGICAL PROCESS 1, 2, 3 27f
29f 4 BASIC PRINCIP 1 – 4

Robert G. Konzelman

MARQUEE
MINISTRY

The Movie Theater
as Church and
Community Forum

HARPER & ROW, PUBLISHERS

New York, Evanston, San Francisco, London

1972

Drawings are by Betty Ellingboe.

The author wishes to acknowledge the permission granted by Columbia Pictures to reproduce two film stills from I NEVER SANG FOR MY FATHER © 1970 by Columbia Pictures and three film stills from CROMWELL © 1970 by Columbia Pictures; and by Warner Bros, Inc. to reproduce the film still from THE LEARNING TREE © 1969 by Warner Bros.-Seven Arts, Inc.

FIRST EDITION

LIBRARY OF CONGRESS CATALOG CARD NUMBER: 73–184215

1972

To Jeanne
the star in my own "Love Story"

CONTENTS

INTRODUCTION

This book is an effort to answer some of the many questions that come to us every week regarding the use of secular films in the educational ministry of the church. Since 1964, when we first began to develop an adult education program making use of various forms of the mass media, these letters have increased from an occasional inquiry to a steady flow. During the past year, 40 to 60 percent of my incoming mail each month has related to the use of films in religious education. Obviously those who seek such information are already convinced that secular films can provide an excellent means of involving both youth and adults in vital awareness regarding themselves and their world as they pursue their religious quest for meaning in life. What they ask for is help in developing ways and means of using them more regularly and effectively. Insights into the meaning and potentials of film in education in our time have outstripped experience with it. Therefore, I offer this contribution to the growing tide of "how to" books.

While I cannot avoid some comment on film history and the techniques of film-making and viewing, this will be only for purposes of illustration. Those who want more details or basic grounding in the art of the film will find better help elsewhere. I shall try to stick to the "how" in the hope that churches of all denominations may find new and better ways of using secular films in the service of the church.

A word of definition is in order. The term secular as employed in the following pages is not intended to mean the opposite of religious. It refers to the sponsorship or origin of the film rather than its content. Thus for our purposes in this volume a secular film is regarded as one *produced by a non-church-related motion picture company as a business enterprise and exhibited commercially primarily to make a profit.* This definition includes but is not limited to the product of the so-called Hollywood motion picture industry. The films I shall be referring to are current pictures whose titles are emblazoned on theater marquees and billboards and advertised on radio and television and in the often lurid theater ads of the daily newspapers.

Every year the Hollywood film industry produces and exhibits between 200 and 300 such pictures. (In 1970 American motion picture companies put out 280 feature films.*) Current expenditures for the production and distribution of secular films in the United States are in excess of one and a quarter billion dollars a year. Simple logic suggests that somewhat more than that is spent at the box office. Estimates are that each week nearly twenty million people in America buy tickets for motion pictures.

If these figures are added to the millions who see reruns of older films on television (it was reported that eighty-six million people viewed the television showing of *Ben Hur* on a single night), the number of persons watching secular films in the United States probably far exceeds those who attend America's churches every week.

On a time basis alone, secular films provide awesome competition for the church in its efforts to engage youth and adults in meaningful experiences of worship and education. But there is more than time involved. There is the question of influence or effect upon those who sit in darkness to receive whatever light the film has to offer. There is a growing awareness today that secular

*"Every Night at the Movies," *Life* magazine, September 7, 1971.

films play a significant role in belief and value formation and reinforcement in our culture. This, plus the fact that millions of its members do see such films each week, makes it a matter of importance for the church to deal responsibly and creatively with them.

On the other hand, these films are in effect multi-million-dollar tools which can be used in its educational ministry (the current average cost of a feature film is $3,300,000). It is my hope that the following pages will help the individual church to make use of this costly tool more frequently.

Lastly, it is hoped that this volume will also assist persons in the film industry to gain a better understanding of the nature and possibilities of their product as a powerful force for good in the life of communities, and that a new alliance may be developed between those who make, distribute, and exhibit secular films and the church.

ROBERT G. KONZELMAN

Minneapolis, Minnesota
August 23, 1971

1. WHY BOTHER?

There is a loud and rising clamor across the nation against current secular film fare because of the excessive portrayal of sex, violence, and other behavior and attitudes inimical to those taught and regarded desirable by the church in our Judeo-Christian culture. In many ways the clamor is justified, and the question might well be asked, "Why bother with secular films?" However, there are two ways of regarding current secular films from the church's point of view. They can be either a negative force or a positive value in our culture. A central thesis of this book will be that the church has the power to help determine which they shall be.

In explaining this thesis it will be helpful for us to look at what has come to be called the "cultural wash" and the processes of erosion and corrosion related to it in the formation of beliefs and values.

Each of us exists within a complex network of influences. Some of these come from our relationships with other people, some from physical surroundings, some from political and economic processes, and others from the ways in which we seek to express ourselves in art forms, recreation, and through the communication media. We cannot escape these influences to matter how hard we try. We are bathed in them daily. They are the very atmosphere of our existence. Our attitudes, beliefs, and values are formed by the countless transactions that take place every day between us and our environment. It is as impossible for us to evade these influences of our society as it is for the river bottom to avoid contact with the river or for an unfilterable virus to be isolated from the atmosphere. Thus the cultural wash sweeps over and about us, molding and shaping us and never leaving us the same.

The importance of all this is intensified today because science and technology have increased the power and changed the character of the social tide that bathes us. Consequently, our beliefs and values are undergoing more rapid and radical change than in any preceding generation.

For instance, there was a time when the cultural influence emanated primarily from home, church, and school. Today science and technology have knocked down all the walls. Man is no longer confined physically or intellectually to these narrow boundaries. He now lives in what Marshall MacLuhan has called a "global village." The electronic media have brought the world into the living room and personal experience of virtually every man, woman, and child. Instant communication is possible, and every conceivable kind of thought, action, belief, and value is almost immediately accessible to us, not only descriptively but pictorially; and all this in a land in which freedom of speech and expression is a basic premise of our corporate life and is being given increasingly broader interpretation. These factors make it impossible, even if it were desirable, to control the input of information and thereby the force or character of the cultural wash as related to the formation or alteration of beliefs and values.

In other words, we are increasingly subjected to influences which may be in conflict with things we have previously known or been taught. This may not necessarily be bad. In fact, it has as much potential for good as for evil. One of the results of "masscom" is that with new information and insights immediately available, beliefs and values may find stronger reinforcement than was possible before. But it also means that beliefs and values may be challenged. Indeed, moving from a more restricted or limited environment to one that has become global with masscom tends to raise more questions related to our beliefs and values than it answers.

A part of the malaise of our times is that most of us live with a vague and haunting sense of uncertainty. We have the feeling that someone has craftily sneaked into our world and switched around all the signposts. The upshot is that we are confused both about where we have been and where we are going. Sometimes we even wonder if there is a destination any more.

One response to this situation is nihilism: a surrender to the status quo and the temptation to despair—to believe that all is meaningless, nothing counts, everything rusts and wastes away—to "say to the mountains, 'Fall on us'; and to the hills, 'Cover us' " (Luke 23:30), and do nothing to improve matters. There can be little doubt that the apocalyptic mood of our times, the emergence of theologies of hope, new emphasis on pentecostalism, the return to religious fundamentalism, the development of the Jesus cult among the youth, are all in some measure a reaction to the threat to beliefs and values occasioned by our new technologies and especially the electronic mass media, all resulting in a deep impulse to get back—or get away—to something sounder and truer.

An inverse alternative, however, is to see in these new technologies the possibility of better opportunities: to accept the threat they pose to our beliefs and values—to struggle with it as did Jacob with the messenger of old, and refuse to let go until we are blessed. This means that we do not withdraw from the changing scene, but use the very things that bring the message of confusion and despair to find our way to more solid ground. Instead of ignoring the mass media, perhaps we can make use of them to enter into dialogue with the technologies and the opposing and contradictory ideas they often bring.

Such an approach would require the church to plant its feet

squarely in the flow of the cultural wash and refuse to be swept downstream or to accept a marginal role in the life of its people. Rather, it would move to their ground and engage them in a dialogue there, using the very media that preoccupy them. I believe this is the way the church can best help its people in a masscom world to avoid the erosion and corrosion of beliefs and values. For the fact is, a responsible church dare not ignore or refuse to employ the mass media in its educational ministry, so crucial a role do they play in the formation of these same beliefs and values. As Moses lifted up the serpent in the wilderness for the healing of the poeple, so the church today must lift up these powerful new media of ours, which if left alone can destroy us, but if raised up can work toward healing.

Let us take a closer look at what is involved in the "erosion and corrosion" of values in the lives of individuals. Those who remember or have read about the dustbowl days of the thirties will have no difficulty in recognizing it. In those years the uncontrolled forces of nature destroyed millions of acres of once-fertile and productive farmland. The rich topsoil was washed or blown away and only the rocky, untillable, infertile subsoil remained. Those who make their living from the land were impoverished and the economy of whole regions of the country was adversely affected.

The same thing can and does happen in the realm of morals, beliefs, and values if the cultural wash is left to itself in the world, to sweep over it at random and unchecked. The continual flow of communication (regardless of its nature or source) which contradicts one's own religious insights and attitudes may well in the end undermine them, and so destroy or diminish their guiding, supporting force. From the church's point of view this not only impoverishes the individual but has a decided effect on the entire culture.

"Corrosion" is caused by chemical change in a substance as a result of exposure to certain elements. It is not always apparent in a changed appearance. A metal tool left in the open for a length of time may still look the same, but when applied, will break without warning from the stress of the very task for which it was designed.

There is a very real parallel to this corrosive action in the realm of beliefs and values. It is difficult over a short span of time to see the direct effect of the cultural wash upon people. Those who do research in this field are hard put to find any one-for-one relationship between forms of activity or conduct witnessed on TV or in movies and the specific acts of an individual. Under influence of the media (and in this case of secular films), individuals may still carry on the formal expression of their values and attitudes. The outward form is maintained in the midst of exposure to elements in the cultural wash which may be quite contrary to them. A person may not even be aware of the weakening effect the culture is having upon him. However, in a time of stress or crisis, his once firmly held values, morals, and beliefs may no longer support him. Perhaps it was to this very process that the author of II Timothy referred when he spoke of certain of his own contemporaries as "holding the form of religion but denying the power of it" (II Tim. 3:5).

So Let's Talk about Film

What I have said above applies to all facets of the mass media. And here I must refer specifically to secular films. Not everyone is in agreement that they really affect the personal beliefs and resultant behavior of individuals. Since they are primarily entertainment, some say that the social and psychological mechanisms at work in all life situations place them beyond the possibility of seriously influencing human behavior. This view is held firmly by many in the film industry itself, especially those involved in the production and distribution of secular films. Jack Valenti, president of the Motion Picture Association of America, has stated it clearly in the following words:

I don't think that the communications media and particularly TV and motion pictures have been responsible for permissiveness in our society for drugs and pills, for mindless violence, for departures from moral and ethical precepts. The media do, and should, mirror what a society is at any time. This is feedback from society itself. It is not a feed-in from the medial to society.*

The question as to whether the mass media lead the culture or follow it in simply reporting out what is already there, has been long and hotly debated. Most persons on the commercial side of the film industry would probably side with Mr. Valenti; though such contact as one has with film industry personnel, from national directors of public relations to small-town theater managers, may give rise to a certain discomfiture with the thesis. What those holding this view do not acknowledge is that there is a cyclical character in the process, for the influence received by any individual from the culture is transmitted through the person back to the culture at a different level. This is why the simplistic view that motion pictures simply reflect the surrounding society is an unacceptable answer to those who criticize secular films. However, whether the industry leads or follows the culture in what it portrays on the screen is not the issue. The question is, Do the mass media (especially secular films) in fact influence the thought and behavior of people? To this query there is evidence that yields a decidedly affirmative answer.

For instance, Esse Campbell refers to this phenomenon in an article which appeared some time ago in *Variety*, a Hollywood trade paper. The headlines of her story score the point with these words: BY CLOTHES-HORSING AROUND FILM FILLIES SET STYLE TRENDS. She recalls how men's underwear manufacturers panicked in 1934 when sales of undershirts dropped drastically after the opening of *It Happened One Night*. In this picture Clark Gable did away with his undershirt, exposing his manly chest, and completely changed American custom as to this item of clothing.

*Reported in *Daily Variety*, 36th Anniversary Edition, p. 8.

It was not until World War II and the emergence of the regulation GI skivvy shirt that American men were retrained to wear undershirts.

In a fascinating volume, Lawrence Langner documents the change of style trends in women's clothes by identifying them with the clothing worn by film personalities such as Gloria Swanson (dramatic femme fatale), Carole Lombard (soft, clinging fabrics and lines inspiring the look of elegance), Joan Crawford (the dolman sleeve), Marlene Dietrich (the first trousers and trousersuits for women), Audrey Hepburn (the Sabrina neckline), to name a few.* More recently the film *Bonnie and Clyde* provided inspiration for a whole line of clothing for both men and women in the fashion of the thirties. Though these examples may seem somewhat less than world-shaking, they do illustrate the power of movies to affect some level of human behavior.

In making the point, it is not my intention to cast secular films in the role of either villain or hero (though there are times when either or both may fit). I simply wish to underscore the fact that, like all forms of mass media, secular motion pictures are not a neutral force in our society. By merely existing, they are "for better or worse"—but never for nothing. This is in part due to the nature and power of film itself as a form of communication, and in part to the psychological and sociological situation of the viewer. Seldom does a person view a film and leave the encounter unchanged.

Is There Any Evidence?

While it is true that researchers find it hard to establish a direct relation between mass media and consequent human behavior, there is much evidence in support of the cultural wash theory. Harold Mendelsohn, director of the Communications Depart-

*Lawrence Langner, *The Importance of Wearing Clothes* (New York: Hastings House, 1959).

ment of the University of Denver and a leading authority in the field, in an impressive book entitled *Mass Entertainment* has provided a cautious and balanced view of its effect on the behavior, values, and beliefs of individuals. In a chapter on the sociological function of the media, he indicates their powerful influence in our society.

. . . the peripheral evidence appears to substantiate the fact that indeed large masses of Americans use "mass entertainment" for social emulation purposes. . . . by its very preoccupation with the middle class, then, mass entertainment reinforces the values in life ways of the middle class and as a by-product no doubt helps to maintain the middle class status quo of American society.

While Mendelsohn refers primarily to the use of mass media for entertainment rather than to their influential content, he does also say:

Movies extend the experiences of the audience vicariously and translate problems which are common to mankind into specific and personal situations with which identification is easy. Results from some preliminary research with audience reactions provide the hypothesis that audiences tend to accept as true that part of a movie story which is beyond their experience. *

If this is so, then it is easy to see how casual sex, negative attitudes toward marriage, dishonesty, and life-styles beyond the experience of the individual may be regarded as desirable, acceptable, or even normative by many and thus encourage or support similar conduct or attitudes in the viewer.

From the foregoing, it may be seen that secular film cannot be ignored by the church. It is, in its own way, tampering with that part of human existence which is a primary province of religion. Because motion pictures in their impact upon individuals are never wholly benign, and do affect for better or for worse the

*Harold Mendelsohn, *Mass Entertainment*, (New Haven: College and University Press, 1966), pp. 67–68, 63.

lives of individuals and the character of our society, they can be ignored by the church only to its peril.

Everybody's Doing It

Now, applying all this to the potentially erosive or corrosive power of films as one element in the cultural wash, it appears that there are two primary factors involved. One is the seeming public endorsement of whatever is displayed or heard in public; the other is the peculiar motivational power of film itself.

We have all discovered, to our joy or sorrow, that we have difficulty putting our finest resolves into action unless there is reinforcement or support from our surroundings. For instance, it is easier to be good when there are people close to us who expect us to be good and who agree with and support our value system or moral standards. On the other hand, when we are among those who permit or encourage thought and behavior contrary to, or different from, our accepted norms, it is easier to violate them. This is another way of saying that our behavior is to a great extent shaped by our surroundings, and the climate of our culture affects our belief and value system both negatively and positively. The idea that "everybody's doing it" has a powerful influence on us for both good and ill. Though what the screen portrays in a given film may be far from true as representing everybody, nevertheless the very fact that "everybody" allows it to be shown creates the illusion of public endorsement and approval. The more frequent the message is given, the stronger the encouragement to imitate it. Thus if the content of current secular films is consistently contrary to the traditional teaching of the church, it is reasonable to believe that an undermining of beliefs and values and a consequent change in moral behavior will take place. On the other hand, if it serves to foster thought and action in accord with the church's teaching, so much the more should the use of secular films be encouraged.

As to the second factor, the power of film itself to sweep a person into the action portrayed and to condition his responses is a formidable element to reckon with, over which the individual is not altogether in control. Feelings are effectively moved by what is seen or implied on the screen. The laughter, tears, groans, and sighs heard in any motion picture theater are ample proof of the capacity of film to stir the emotions. Because of the psychological dynamics at work in us, this is evidence that we do, experience vicariously what is portrayed on the screen. Sometimes not even what is said or seen but what is implied has the most seductive motivational power over the individual.

Films provide the individual with a wraparound culture in which he may find that he is capable of doing, thinking, and saying many things he would never otherwise have regarded as possible. But what is even more devastating, it may well reduce the threshold of his tolerance; some of his moral strength and resolve will have been washed away by the vicarious experience. This potency of the film, coupled with the illusion that "everybody's doing it," may over a period of time produce an erosive or corrosive element in terms of the kinds of behavior, beliefs, and values approved and advocated by the church.

The pervasive and potentially destructive power of secular films has, since the turn of the century, aroused certain responses in the church. These have fallen primarily into two classes, both of which are based on the premise that motion pictures are—by and large—a negative influence on the culture. One tactic has been to ignore the film industry in the hope that somehow it would "go away." The other has been to try to control its product by censorship and/or boycott (the next chapter will take a brief look at what has happened in this respect over the years and make an alternative proposal).

As to the ostrich approach, regardless of how hard we try, we cannot filter the secular motion picture and its influence out of the cultural wash by ignoring it, for a whole variety of reasons. First, the people who act in, produce, and direct these films are celebrities in America. They are big news, a formidable part of the image equipment of our society. In a very real sense they become folk heroes who exert a subtle and mystical influence over young and old. A classic example, duplicated in many ways ever since, is an incident that took place back in 1910. Even by that time, movie personalities had already become folk heroes. A rumor went out that actress Florence Lawrence had died. When the people of St. Louis learned that the reports were false they were overjoyed, and hearing of their concerned reaction, Miss Lawrence made a personal appearance in the city. A larger crowd turned out to meet her than had greeted William Howard Taft, then President of the United States, the week before.

Moreover, the phenomenon of what might be called media-spillover gives these film folk-heroes and the vehicles that carry them to prominence a kind of omnipresence. Try as you like, you cannot eliminate them from the cultural wash. You may choose not to see movies, but you cannot escape being confronted by stories about film people in newspapers and magazines, seeing them on billboards, and both hearing and seeing them over radio and TV. In addition, you will doubtless be confronted by some-one or something related to current film properties through pictures and endorsements of products ranging from breakfast cereals to automobiles. In other words, in our global village the gossip gets around. You simply cannot go untouched by what the mass media have to say about Hollywood's latest and greatest. And what the people and products of the Hollywood film industry say and do in their private lives, as well as on film, does inevitably influence our culture.

Thus, even though the church may for all outward purposes appear to ignore the film industry, this is clearly a self-delusion and a deception. Official action, whether silence or pronouncement, is not the church in reality. The church is its people, and they are everywhere, even among the twenty million who buy tickets to motion picture theaters every week in this country. Whether pastors and church boards want to acknowledge it or not, their people do see a great number of films. This is especially true of the younger generation. A study made in 1970 indicated that 59 percent of all theater tickets sold in the United States in the previous year were purchased by persons under twenty-five years of age. There was also a noticeable increase in the number of people over twenty-five attending the movies.

All this is in addition to the entrance of the film industry into private homes by way of the television screen. *Look* magazine has reported that, in a week in the New York area, 258 hours (equivalent to more than ten solid 24-hour days) of films were shown on television. During the same week, in the Los Angeles area, 233 films were screened. No one, therefore, can reasonably deny that the film industry, through its product and people is a significant part of our culture, and even the church cannot ignore it out of existence or curtail its influence. Current secular films simply have to be dealt with by a responsible church.

Moreover, such films are costly, effective, and available tools which the church can use in its educational ministry. It is hard to imagine that any creative church would want to ignore them.

Conclusion

To summarize what I have been saying as to why the church should bother with this problem, I quote Dr. F. Thomas Trotter, dean of the School of Theology, Claremont, California:

We are now painfully aware of the fact that students entering graduate schools today are children of the television age. Their world is mediated by moving pictures, not primarily by books. Their perceptions are symbolized in visual imagery. They probably are harbingers of the future. Knowledge will increasingly be mediated by visual—i.e., filmic—events. Therefore, the church has an extraordinary responsibility to its people to educate for cinematic experience. What is needed is not primarily some dogmatic apparatus that will reassure churchmen that such and such a film is "safe." The church of the future will simply refuse to believe such data. What is needed is a new sense of style and discrimination that will enable the church adequately to apprehend and criticize the film. Unless the church can educate its people to the issues of discrimination in film experience, it will have nothing to say to its people in regard to the dominant mode of communication of ideas and values. If the latter is the case, then an entire section of contemporary human social experience will be untouched by the reflection of the church. The important question, then, is not "SHALL the church involve itself in the film?" but "HOW shall it involve itself in the film? *

Or as the poet Carl Sandburg has said, in oft-quoted words which lucidly express the awareness that underlies every page of this book:

I meet people occasionally who think motion pictures, the product Hollywood makes, is merely entertainment, has nothing to do with education. That's one of the darndest fool fallacies that is current. . . . Anything that brings you to tears by way of drama does something to the deepest roots of our personality. All movies, good or bad, are educational and Hollywood is the foremost educational institution on earth. What, Hollywood more important than Harvard? The answer is not as clean as Harvard, but nevertheless farther reaching.

Why, then, use secular films in the service of the church?

1. A responsible church cannot ignore them, because in our culture they play a determinative role in belief and value formation.

2. A creative church will not want to ignore them, in view of their great potential as an educational tool.

*"The Church Moves Toward Film Discrimination," Reprint from *Religion in Life* (Summer, 1969)

2. THE CHURCH AND
THE SECULAR FILM INDUSTRY

If it is true that we must relate to the film industry in significant ways, an important question arises: namely, *how* do you relate to an industry to strong and diffuse, whose power centers seem so far removed from the local parish and whose product is so often offensive to the moral sensibilities of many in the church?

Granted that much of current film output is technically, culturally, and artistically inferior, and possibly detrimental to the moral and spiritual welfare of our people—yet it must be admitted that not everything viewed with alarm within and outside the church is morally or theologically objectionable. Much of the apprehension results from inadequate understanding of the changes that have taken place in our world at all levels of human existence, compounded by ignorance of film as a form of communication in an ever increasingly visual culture. But leaving these particular matters for the moment, let us address ourselves to the question of how it is possible to relate to the world of secular films so that their negative influence on the culture can be minimized and their positive potential made use of in the church's educational ministry.

A variety of answers have been brought forth over the years. For purposes of this chapter, we can lump them together under

14

the three words, control, consent, and cooperation. These represent alternatives open to us in trying to find a way of relating to the film industry.

The Effort to Control

Effort to regulate the film industry from the outside has been continuous on the part of the church almost from the very beginning of film-making. In 1915 the Supreme Court of the United States, as a result of a suit brought by the Motion Picture Distributors, ruled that most pictures were not entitled to the full guarantees of the First Amendment of the Constitution. From that time until 1952, censorship of all films—not only the questionable ones—was practiced throughout the United States. However, in 1952 the Supreme Court reversed the decision of 1915, granting motion pictures the full guarantees of the First and Fourteenth Amendments, which deal with freedom of speech and of the press. Since that time obscenity has been the only standard that can be applied by any board of censorship to determine whether or not a film may be publicly exhibited. In 1961 the Supreme Court again defined the issue by ruling that a requirement of prior submission of a motion picture to a board of censors would be legal only if strict safeguards were observed. The proposed safeguards follow:

A. The burden of proof that the film is not protected by the First Amendment must rest with the censor.

B. The final decision to ban the picture must be that of the court—not the censor board.

C. The burden of instituting legal proceedings rests with the censor, who must either issue a license or secure from the courts an injunction against exhibition.

D. These procedures must take place in the shortest possible time.

Any censorship law since 1961 not providing for these safe-guards has been regarded as unconstitutional. Though the battle of censorship has continued to the present, the right of films to share the full freedom enjoyed by other forms of the mass media has gradually come to be accepted.

Facing such a prestigious bulwark as the Supreme Court of the United States defending the right of films to be heard and seen, the church has tried in various ways to exercise a code of censor-ship of its own, operating mainly on the premise of boycott or negative publicity. In 1934 the Catholic Legion of Decency was formed. It sought to classify films, placing a ban upon those not judged acceptable in the eyes of the church. This movement was supported by many Protestant and Jewish groups.

However, the Catholic Legion of Decency no longer exists as such, having been superseded by the National Catholic Office of Motion Pictures. Though this agency still exercises a censorship role, its main thrust is in film classification, evaluation, and educa-tion. From the primarily negative stance of the old Catholic Le-gion of Decency, the Roman Catholic Church through NCOMP has moved to a position of unquestioned leadership in film edu-cation among religious groups in the United States.

Some Protestant groups—most conspicuously the National Council of Churches, through its Broadcasting and Film Com-mission (BFC)—have tried to influence the film industry by get-ting in touch with or in some way ministering to people who work in it, and by providing script review and consultative services on the content of films. For the most part, however, this approach has also been ineffective. All such efforts have failed to influence the essential content of motion pictures in any significant mea-sure. Films have become increasingly frank and exceedingly vio-lent. And the basic reason rests in the fact that sex and violence continue to make money, and that is what the film industry is really all about.

This was illustrated for the author recently in a personal con-versation with a vice president of one of the major film companies in Hollywood. Responding to comments about the need for films which support or at least do not undermine beliefs and values proclaimed by the churches, he said, "We honestly would like to make better films, but there are the stockholders, and like it or not, we have to make money for them."

The motion picture industry is first and foremost a commercial enterprise. For instance, it has a capital investment of over 3 billion dollars in theaters alone, another 150 million in studios, and 24 million in distribution facilities. It has a gross income of over 1.3 billion dollars (nearly half the amount spent on all other spectator entertainments and sports in the United States). The industry exists to make a profit for its stockholders by providing entertainment for those who are willing to pay for it. In this fact, and this alone, lies the reason why all attempts by the church to control it from the outside, whether by censorship, boycott, or moral persuasion, must inevitably fail. But also in this simple fact lies the secret of how to get better films, of which more later.

Because the film industry is in a great measure protected by laws that guarantee its right to speak, and because it is self-admittedly an entertainment medium existing for profit, its pressure on our culture will continue in whatever direction the people who spend their money at the box office want it to go. All of which is to say that secular films will remain a vital force in the cultural wash of America, and for better or worse we shall continue to be bathed in it, regardless of the direction in which its influence runs.

There is at present increasing concern for some form of censorship of secular films. Where the church should take its stand in the current clamor is a question of serious dimensions which must be thought through very, very carefully. Needless to say, the film industry has given this much attention, and for many years.

As an effort to forestall the cry for public censorship and control, it has sought to discipline itself through its self-administered production and advertising codes. In November of 1968, the Motion Picture Association of America announced a new code and rating program. The purpose was to rate American and foreign films according to their suitability for specific audiences. It hoped in this way to allow the public to determine what it wanted or did not want to see. The rating symbols selected were:

G: All ages admitted—general audience.

GP: *   All ages admitted—parental guidance suggested.

R: Restricted—under 17 requires accompanying parent or adult guardian.

X: No one under 17 admitted—age level may vary in certain areas.

Theoretically and in principle the system is intelligent and responsible. The plan won the support (in principle) of the two major agencies representing American Christendom's concerns for the public media: the Broadcasting and Film Commission of the National Council of Churches and the National Catholic Office for Motion Pictures. However, by the spring of 1970 it was clear to these agencies that all was not going well with the rating system. They published a joint statement indicating that instead of rating films as to their overall quality, the ratings were related only to the film's suitability for children. It also produced evidence that exhibitors were not uniformly or consistently enforcing the suggested limitations and that children were in fact being admitted to R- and X-rated films in many theaters. The report also pointed up the tendency of the raters to judge a film's suitability on the basis of explicit language and visual impact only, with little regard for the values implicit in the film. It claimed, on the contrary, that even if no "overt" adult material or profane language is present in a film, its manner of treatment may be such as to require its placement in the R category rather than GP. The statement also said, ". . . The two church film agencies sense a new public sympathy for public censorship which can only result

*In January 1972 the MPAA changed this symbol to PG as a more accurate designation for Parental Guidance.

in a restriction of the responsible exchange of ideas in our society."

After outlining several actions that might be taken by the film industry itself to avoid external censorship, the report concluded with these words: "The motion picture industry has very little time to make these changes voluntarily before public clamor for censorship secures legal sanctions which could be extremely harmful, both to the industry and to public welfare."

These statements clearly indicate a reluctance on the part of the two national church agencies to see film censorship become a necessity in America.

The story is not yet complete. On May 18, 1971 the BFC and NCOMP issued another joint statement withdrawing their support from the rating system as then functioning. The reason given was that the suggestions for improvement made in the first statement had not been acted upon, and that in fact they regarded the ratings as even less reliable in the spring of 1971 than they had been a year before.

In withdrawing support for the industry's rating system, the two agencies nonetheless reaffirmed their belief that freedom from censorship is eminently preferable and desirable, but that self-regulation by the industry is vital if it is to be preserved. They said, "It is essential that the motion picture industry itself realize that it must develop a workable, dependable, and credible system of self-regulation as an alternative to governmental censorship."

The position of the church as indicated in the above statements is in fact a refusal, for political and theological reasons, to join in any public clamor for film censorship—a refusal which supports every effort to encourage the film industry to act responsibly and to seek out effective means of self-regulation. For one thing as indicated, the reason for such a position rests in the First and Fourteenth Amendments of the United States Constitution, which guarantees the right of free speech and the "responsible exchange of ideas in our society." It ought to be clear that once these safeguards to individual freedom of speech and thought are abrogated for anyone, the way is open to the control of all forms of mass media and freedom of speech, and the church itself may lose its freedom to proclaim its message. The church is, therefore, jeopardizing its own political and religious freedoms if it supports movements that deny any segment of the population the right to speak.

But theologically also, it is against the spirit of the Gospel to try to control by law that which should be an opportunity to proclaim the grace of God. The position of the church, therefore, ought to be clear in its efforts not to control the film industry by law and censorship, but to find a more creative way to influence the content of secular film.

The Matter of Consent

What, then, can be said of the second alternative for influencing the film industry, here called "consent"? As averred earlier, the church cannot ignore the film industry out of existence, for there will always be those in society willing to pay to see bad films. For concerned persons simply to pay no attention to them is actually a way of consenting to their continued production.

What is really needed is the positive support of the film industry in its effort to make better pictures. However, thereby hangs a tale. It is the persistent testimony of people in the business that whenever it has tried to produce and market the kinds of films that society, and especially the church, say they really want, it has with few exceptions lost money. Because of this, the industry does not take the church seriously in its demand for good films. Here again, then, by ignoring good and bad films alike, the church is really encouraging the film industry in taking the path of least resistance—i.e., in pursuit of the quickest buck—by pandering to the baser human appetites and producing films that negate the cherished ideals of the Christian community.

If the church is to influence the content of secular films in any significant way, it must determine to let its Yea be Yea, and its Nay a real Nay. If it is going to avoid bad films, then it must also support the good ones—otherwise it consents by default to the wrong pictures. The industry is going to make money, one may be sure. It is the author's conviction that it would rather do it by putting out a good product, but if it can't, it will not hesitate to make a profit in any way it can. Thus the real task before the church is to help give the film industry a way of making money by producing better films. This is the only way we will ever get them, for the problem is treatable only through economic sanctions (which can be positive as well as negative)—a fact which brings us to the third alternative, the proposal of this book: that of cooperation.

Cooperation

By suggesting that the church cooperate with the motion picture industry as a more adequate way of relating to it, I am not advising any direct role in the business of producing, distributing, or exhibiting secular films. I am simply suggesting the planned and programmatic use of some of the better films where and when they appear in the local community. If this seems naïvely simple, that may be because in fact it is so. But if it catches on, it may be just simple enough to exert a profound influence on the shape of our culture, while serving the educational needs of the church and the economic requirements of the film industry.

Cooperation means that what is done has to work for the good of everyone involved, in terms of their own reasons for being. Anything short of this is exploitation. This is primarily what has been wrong in many previous efforts on the part of the church to influence the film product, and on the part of the film industry to secure the church's support at the box office. Neither has come to terms with the other's reason for being, and each has seen the other as either an enemy or a subject to be exploited.

It is time that both church and industry should ask new questions. Instead of "How can we get them to serve *our* purposes?" we in the church need to ask, "How can we help the film industry to attain its objectives at the same time as it helps us in the performance of our educational ministry?" The film industry needs to ask, "How can we help the church to its ultimate goals while making money through film production and distribution?"

I submit that, by beginning here, it is possible for the church to get better educational tools and opportunities—in other words, more useful films—and for the film industry to produce the kind of films that people, including the church, really want, and thus make a mutual *positive* contribution to the culture that washes incessantly over us.

There can be no doubt that widespread use of secular films by the church does make a difference at the box office. In a letter I received from Robert S. Ferguson, vice-president of Columbia Pictures Corporation, he commented on the effect of the work done by the Department of Parish Education of the American Lutheran Church in connection with the film, *Guess Who's Coming to Dinner.* In the letter he said in part, "Thank you especially for the wonderful job you and the American Lutheran Church are doing in connection with 'Guess Who's Coming to Dinner.' It may interest you to know that the picture is one of the most successful ever released in the United States, and *I am sure that the work of your Division of Parish Education has a great deal* to do with its success." (italics mine).

Robert Thill of ABC North Central Theaters, Inc. in a letter dated August 17, 1967, comments, "We advised our theater managers to contact your pastors and they were most cooperative. As a result, the motion picture 'Up the Down Staircase' was a box office success in every town."

From Merle J. Burns, theater manager in Menno, South Dakota: "We have been getting fine results from the Lutheran Church Study Guide Program. The local minister organizes the churches in the area and they come in groups to see selected pictures."

From Ray Vonderhaar, president of the National Association of Theater Owners of the North Central States: "Any exhibitor who hasn't used this [the Dialogue Thrust in Films program] to his own benefit will have a pleasant surprise because this is the most effective promotion available. It is contact with the group of people we have tried so long to reach."

In a report from Bob Scott of ABC North Central Theaters, it was stated that they had followed suggestions of the Division of Parish Education of the American Lutheran Church and made use of their study guide for *The Learning Tree*. As a result, *The Learning Tree* turned out to be one of the top grossers of the year for us in Mitchell."

From these statements it should be clear that the church can make a difference at the box office. When responsible films are recognized and widely used by the church, there can be no doubt that greater effort on the part of the film industry to capture the church audience with a better product will emerge. Most of us learn quickest in connection with our own self-interest, and the film industry is no exception.

If the church really uses the good product, then we will be exercising constructive sanctions and the message to the industry will get through. This, I believe, is the kind of positive, open, honest, and helpful approach a responsible church must take in the future, as it seeks better tools for its tasks and better opportunities to help people develop a discriminating awareness in the realm of beliefs and values.

3. DIALOGICAL FILM STUDY

Neil P. Hurley in his recent book *Theology Through Film* makes our point for us in the following words:

My one objective is to impress on theologians, educators, and representatives of the major world religions that for tens of millions of people the motion picture experience enjoys a psychological and pedagogical legitimacy that has not yet been matched by a corresponding effectiveness in the modes of religious communication.*

In succeeding chapters, various ways of making use of secular films in the service of a church will be discussed. All are valid and desirable in terms of the purposes for which they are planned, and there is no single approach that is best in all situations. However, one method which I feel can be of great benefit to the church is what might be called dialogical film study. It is probably the most far-reaching and helpful approach in dealing with the effects of this phase of the cultural wash on the individual's belief and value system.

A Definition

What is dialogical film study, and how does it differ from other efforts to make use of secular films? In what way is it so desirable for religious education?

*New York: Harper & Row, 1970, p. 12.

24

Film study takes many forms. Much of the emphasis in high schools and colleges as well as in film societies and clubs of all descriptions is focused on the film as art. A good deal of attention is given to the internal language through which the message of a moving picture is communicated; image, continuity, structural rhythm, sound, framing, visual and audio effects, etc., become focal points for study and discussion. Others focus on the history of film or on technical aspects of making pictures. Another approach is based on the *auteur* theory: a study of particular film "authors" based on the view that the director is, in his medium, as distinctive in terms of style and skill as the author of a literary work. There is an effort to understand film in terms of the subtleties of the director's personality, viewpoints, etc.

While all these approaches have their own value, they tend to make the film an end in itself. As Hamlet exclaimed, "The play's the thing," so these proclaim that the film's the thing. A film thus becomes an object to be studied, evaluated, praised, or blamed. The process is highly cognitive and often becomes an intellectual game, having nothing to do with beliefs or values in the realm of morals.

Dialogical film study, on the other hand, approaches motion pictures as a communication out of and to our culture. A film is regarded as the effort of some person, group, or even the culture itself to communicate with mankind. Its significance therefore goes beyond its own limits. It is a means and not an end. Its importance to the culture and its effects on our belief and value system are not distilled in Oscars nor do they come to an end when the coveted golden statuettes are distributed at the Academy Awards program. As a fragrance or a stench, the film communication lingers in our cultural atmosphere long after the picture has been deposited in the storage vaults of the producers. Thus in dialogical film study the communication's the thing—not the picture itself as an art object. Here the important element is the film as experienced by the viewer and discussed in terms of meanings. In other words, this type of study is concerned not only with the film and its communication, but with the shared experience of a group of people in relation to it. This is a group activity centered in a filmic experience through which

   —feelings and information are shared,
   —the question of meaning as related to beliefs and values is explored,
   —issues are defined,
   —the individual is affirmed,
   —responsible decisions are encouraged, and
   —openness to the future is fostered.

In the Beginning Was the Film . . .

The starting point for such study is not in books, articles, speeches about film, film reviews, or descriptions, but is the film itself as the heart of a shared experience of a group of people. This occurs when an appropriate film appears in the normal course of events in a local community and people gather together to see it and discuss their common experience. Though seeing and discussing a current film may happen by accident or without benefit of clergy, I am speaking here of making it a planned part of the youth and adult education program of a parish—as much a part as the Sunday sermon or Bible class.

Many films pass through our communities every year, making their deposit in the cultural wash with or without our permission or awareness. Some are of such stature that, like the burning bush to Moses, they can be the occasion for calling people aside to ponder. Certainly God was using an unusual and compelling method to intrude into Moses' sheep-tending activities, that day in the wilderness. And again today, God may need a modern variety of burning bush to attract attention and make men halt in their frenetic pursuits to ask, "What's it all about, Alfie?" It is my belief that some secular films may just succeed in being for many twentieth-century people a counterpart of the ancient sign and wonder, serving the same purpose for the people of God in our time: an event, an occasion, a compelling opportunity to ponder, question, explore—above all, to discover who and what they are, and where, at this point in history, they are heading.

In dialogical film study, the movie itself plays a dual role. It is first of all a catalyst for bringing a group of people together in a learning situation. This is not to minimize the film in any way. Nor is it simply a gimmick to get people to talk together in groups. Rather, we are taking a specific film very seriously as a cultural communication, an "event" in a community—one through which the Most High God may find a means of speaking.

If one seeks a theological rationale for this type of study, perhaps it may best be found in the concept of film as event. Events have always served to focus the religious questing of man. "What does this mean?" was the cry raised at Pentecost. Things happen, and men ask "Why?" . . . "What does it mean?" . . . "What am I to do about it?" Commonplace as the present means may seem, it is true here as in more unusual human happenings that at the juncture of event and question, and man's reflection about the event, the possibility of revelation is born and man is opened to change. God, Lord of all history, is always acting; but at certain critical moments man, as he stops to ponder life, is moved to ask the question of meaning.

In the divine-human encounter that ensues, God speaks to guide and direct him. In other words, through the dialogical situation, triggered by an event, God's word for man may be heard, clarified, believed, and become the basis of action. So—mundane as it may sound—a secular film, possibly a burning bush in its own way, has the potential of being theologically significant, even a means of grace.

The catalytic effect of the film event is only one of its functions in the dialogical process. It is doubtful that film used only as a catalyst would be more than an elaborate and costly visual aid. Its second role has to do with the power of a well-executed film to plunge the viewer into experiences that focus his attention and compel his emotional and intellectual involvement. The artistry and language of the motion picture and the physical situation in which it is viewed draw one vicariously into the action.

In a film, as in no other situation save a dream, time is compressed, cause and effect observed, identification made—but for the viewer, judgment is suspended. In the reprieve from the sentence the film provides, man may be opened to the converting, redeeming word that comes from the picture itself or through the miracle of dialogue that follows. It is to this intimate, wraparound experience and impact that Neil Hurley alludes when he speaks of a "psychological and pedagogical legitimacy that has not yet been matched by a corresponding effectiveness in the modes of religious education."*

And Then There Was the Group

In dialogical film study, the group is as important as the film itself. That stress upon the group and its value to the total filmic experience is what most distinguishes this form of film study from other efforts. Where the film's the thing, the process is highly individualistic and impersonal. But where the communication's the thing, the process is group-oriented and interpersonal, or if you will, communal. In this case, film as communication (both means and message) finds its ultimate role in bringing about "community."

The significance of this for religious education should be obvious. The church is, by definition, the "communion of saints." It is a fellowship at a deep level, a level of self-revelation, of trust, of interdependence, of shared beliefs and values. In our mobile, never-have-a-minute world, there is so very little opportunity for people really to commune with one another beneath the surface of daily trivia. We need shared experiences that have the poten-

*Neil P. Hurley, *Theology Through Film*, (New York: Harper & Row, 1970), p. 12.

[handwritten annotations in top margin: "opening us up / visual media - esp drama + art = feeling vs cognitive"]

tial for opening us up to each other. This is one of the great pluses of the visual media, especially drama and art, which find us at the feeling level rather than the purely cognitive.

Film has this power to create community. It reaches us at the feeling level. When we feel something together, barriers are broken down and we are almost immediately ready for a quality of togetherness and communion that might never exist otherwise. In the interchange that takes place when individuals come together in dialogical film study, insights may be born or deepened regarding an issue or issues; but equally important, people may be opened up to others, to new ways of thinking—about issues, about other people, and about themselves. Since one of the purposes of the church is to express and experience community at meaningful levels, we have here a superb tool at our disposal.

Communication in Dialogue

Four basic principles of communication need to be understood for our film study to have enduring value. (For a full treatment of the nature, purpose, and effect of dialogue see Reuel Howe's book, *Miracle of Dialogue.**)

1. The first purpose of communication is to share information and meaning. This involves making available to people in various ways the knowledge and experience of others at other times and places: their beliefs, hopes, values, truths, behavior, etc. In our dialogical form of film study, the primary means of doing this is the film itself. It may present historical or fictional situations or characters, but the beliefs, attitudes, actions, and viewpoints conveyed usually have a basis in real life. They exist—at least at first —in the mind or experience of the writer of the story or those who have produced the film, and are given form and expression

*New York: Seabury Press, 1963.

through the persons and experiences portrayed. So the film provides information and a viewpoint.

Those involved in a film study all receive this information from it. However, they each receive it in a different way, depending on their own background, knowledge, experience, personality, and a host of other factors. As they react to the message of the film, they share their experience and feelings; this, too, becomes a part of the information input—or, if you will, the content of the film study situation. So the first communication step in any film study is to share reactions, ideas, feelings, and viewpoints without making any judgments.

2. The second purpose of communication here is to encourage one another to make responsible decisions. Whether the decisions agree is unimportant, so long as they are made and accepted by others in the group for what they are. Response is essential. The direction it takes is not.

People often do not understand this and want to insist on only one answer or viewpoint, feeling that anyone who does not accept it must be wrong. This is seen when individuals in a film study group ask questions that imply a right or wrong answer, a judgment of good or bad, as final and absolute. In inquiring as to reactions it is more appropriate to use questions like, "How did you feel about_____?" or "In what ways do you agree with _____?" Such questions invite decision from the person questioned without calling for a definitive judgment on the character whose conduct or words are portrayed in the film, or on earlier comments among the group. Moral judgments on others are not important; decisions regarding oneself, one's feelings and attitudes, are.

It is not inappropriate, however, or destructive of the dialogical process, if one tries to help another person make sure his reaction is really what he says it is. One can do this by pressing the issue with further questions, recalling other persons, scenes, etc., from the film. In this way a person may be led to test his conclusion or gain new insights that will change it and so be enabled to grow.

3. A third purpose of communication is to restore the tension between what is and what has been or might be. So often life becomes dull, commonplace, unexciting as we go through the patterns and forms we have accepted or been forced into. People resent change because it creates tension; but creative tension is essential to growth and to life itself. Tension does not necessarily mean conflict, even though it may bring it about. What it does is point to new ways of acting and thinking instead of following the easy ways or forms learned long ago, and now so familiar as to be automatic.

In this respect films can be exceedingly helpful. We see ourselves as we enter vicariously into the story. The film gives us a showcase for our own lives, emotions, and ideas as we identify with the thoughts, people, places, and situations in it. They can therefore provide the creative tension we need to change and grow and transform. This possibility is heightened when we enter a dialogical situation that is nonjudgmental but calls for decision and acceptance.

4. A fourth purpose of communication is to bring people together as persons in their own right as they seek to know and do the truth, serving God, their fellow men, and themselves. Every human being has a basic need to be recognized as a person in his own right, and not because he holds a particular view or subscribes to a certain system or definition. It is often difficult to grant this acceptance to others in the midst of the business of daily living—or for that matter, to find it for ourselves. But through film study in a dialogical setting, we are given the chance to relate to other people in and through certain issues that are outside us. We neither have to agree with the other persons nor reject them if they disagree with us. Their feeling and views in relation to the film are as valid as ours. It is their experience that confronts us, and it is just as irrefutable as our own. We can

therefore grant the other person or persons the right to be who they are and what they are.

Thus one may learn how to actualize dialogical relationships with others in the real issues of life as it is lived outside the filmic experience, and be strengthened through the encounter.

4. A STRATEGY FOR
SELECTION OF SECULAR FILMS

I want to stress at the outset that I am not suggesting a blanket, unquestioning endorsement of all secular films. I do suggest a *very* selective use of such films in the ongoing educational ministry of the parish. Nor do I have in mind waiting until a good film is made available in 16mm. format for private screening in the church, but rather sending people to the local theater when it makes its normal run. It is important, therefore, that educational leaders develop a strategy for selecting films for use in the parish program. What pictures should be used, frequency of use, method of use, promotional and supporting structures, and so forth, all need to be considered very carefully. As much care and concern should be given to this as to other phases of the church's program. A significant experience with a single film may be more highly instructive and motivating in the lives of some persons than almost anything else the church does.

What are the chief factors in developing a film-use strategy in the parish?

1. Opportunities Available

Obviously the number of opportunities for viewing current secular films will have a bearing on how much can be done. In rural areas or small towns there are fewer chances than in metropolitan centers. On the other hand, the cooperation of the film exhibitor may be greater in a small town because of the lack of competition. The following paragraphs must therefore be interpreted in terms of one's specific situation.

2. Criteria of Selection for Secular Films to be Used by the Church

Many in both the church and the film industry are confused as to what the church can use in films. They tend to think only in terms of biblical pictures, bathrobe dramas, or nice stories with happy endings and an obvious moral. It should be understood that films do not have to be obviously religious (dealing with explicitly religious truths, events, and people, etc.) to be used in dialogical film study in a church program. More often they will not be. Rather, they will be films which present a slice of real life, dealing with the existing dilemmas, decisions, fears and frustrations, joys and sorrows of real people living in a real world. For many reasons, usable secular films are not numerous. Of the approximately three hundred offered to the American public each year, perhaps less than 20 percent at present could be regarded as in any way potentially useful to the church. How, then, does one sort out those worthy of including in the church's educational program?

One way might be to use films selected for special acclaim or study-guide treatment by a denominational film program, such as the Dialogue Thrust in Films Program of the American Lutheran Church,* or some other agency specifically involved in the educational use of films such as Mass Media Ministries** or the St. Clements Film Association.*** Additional criteria for selection should include: *relevance, integrity, quality, availability,* and *timing.*

Relevance

Does the film deal with issues, situations, or problems which are current, with which the constituency to be served is or ought to be concerned—taking into account the limited time and resources available to both the institution and the people it serves? It is a basic principle of education that people learn most willingly and best when the learning opportunity responds to some need the individual has in his own personal life. The task of getting them involved in any kind of a learning experience is difficult or easy according to its relation to the needs and interests of the people concerned. Involvement in film study does not differ in this respect. Relevance is of extreme importance if you are going to engage people in a meaningful film experience.

Integrity

Does the film deal honestly with its subject matter, keeping emphasis on all aspects of the story in appropriate balance? There is currently an increasing use of sex, violence, and crude language in films, which often seem to have no other purpose than to shock, titillate, or pander to the voyeuristic proclivities of the population. This does not mean that any portrayal of vio-

---

*Division of Parish Education, The American Lutheran Church, 422 S. Fifth St., Minneapolis, Minnesota 55435
**Mass Media Ministries, 2116 North Charles Street, Baltimore, Maryland 21218
***St. Clements Film Association, 423 West 46th. St., New York, New York 10036

lence, nudity, or sex is necessarily undesirable or morally wrong. Sometimes these things are necessary if the film is to deal honestly with its subject matter. Integrity in this case would seem to demand explicitness in whatever is being portrayed; it may be as wrong to leave sex, violence, nudity, or bad language out of the film as it would be to include it where it does not belong, or emphasize it out of proportion to other aspects of the picture or its essential message. Integrity as it relates to rough language and other elements is not a question of their mere presence or absence but of their proportion and the reasons for including them.

Integrity is not an easy matter to pin down. Nonetheless, the effectiveness of a film will be in direct proportion to the honesty with which its content is handled.

Quality

Is the film artistically and technically within the limits of good cinema? One need not be a film technician, film buff, or have a master's degree in cinema to know when a picture is technically and artistically acceptable. In this regard we have been much tutored by television.

Though most of us could not articulate what good art or good film technology is, we know it when we see it. It either "gets to us" or it doesn't. The extent to which it affects feelings or thoughts is a measure of its technical and artistic skill. Our tastes have been subtly conditioned over the years to a level of excellence that makes it necessary for a film one is expected to take seriously to reach a minimum level of artistic and technical execution.

If you have any doubt about this, simply watch a rerun of a Hollywood film of 1940 or the early fifties and compare your reactions to it with your feelings about current movies or major television shows. Usually you will think of the earlier film—unless it was an exception—as sophomoric and "corny."

Though tastes may differ, some minimum standard of art and technical skill must be present in a film that is expected to have educational value.

Availability and Timing

Will a film be available in the community at an appropriate time and place? Sometimes a picture loses its potential usefulness because it is not to be had when a particular message is most relevant. In the spring and summer of 1970 the film *Z* was being shown in some communities. It came at a time of great hue and cry for law and order and rigid control. Some were crying "Facism!" to efforts of the government to impress order on communities. *Z* would have made an excellent study program, with great potential, rightly used, to bring both sides of the question together for discussion of the issues. However, for various reasons it was not booked in many communities. It therefore lost a splendid opportunity to be instructive and forceful in guiding the thought of people at a very critical time in history. To say nothing of missing its box office potential!

Sometimes the exigencies of the film distribution business itself makes a picture unavailable for maximum use. In the city of Minneapolis in the fall of 1968, there was a major attempt to deal with a racial crisis. Religious and social agencies struggled to find ways to bring people together, to focus attention on some of the basic issues in race relations. An effort was made to have the films *Guess Who's Coming to Dinner* and *In the Heat of the Night* play simultaneously in theaters throughout the Twin Cities area, and to organize theater discussion programs and home and neighborhood groups so that the problems presented in these films could be talked about after viewing them. These very issues were being faced in the Twin Cities at the time.

Everyone liked the idea, including those who owned and managed the theaters; but existing contracts and agreements with film distributors and exhibitors made it impossible to put the plan into operation. Thus the availability of a film at the right time and place to gain necessary involvement is of vital importance.

However, it is sometimes possible to bring a film back into a community after it has run there. A case in point is the excellent *"Nobody Waved Goodbye.* This movie went through the Twin Cities without a ripple the first time. But the committee for a Youth Education Conference at the University of Minnesota arranged to use it in its program on a rental basis. Religious educators who saw it went back to their communities and asked local theater managers to book it. The distributor received calls from all over the state for booking dates, and the film made more money on its rerun than when it opened.

Whether the criteria presented above or others are used, some selection strategy is necessary for good use of secular films in the parish. One cannot just take potluck and expect successful results.

3. Frequency of Use

Like any other educational method, film study has its limitations as well as advantages. Secular films are not an educational panacea. They will not meet every educational need and ought not to be used simply as a gimmick to obtain participation. Any educational method or tool can become dull by overuse or misuse. Strategy for film utilization therefore presupposes an affirmative answer to the question, "Is a secular film the most appropriate medium to use in terms of the purpose of the learning experience being planned?"

The number of films selected each year will vary on the basis of the goals and purposes of the film study effort. It should not be thought that fertile use of secular films in the service of the church requires a great number of them. A few good film experiences each year will have a significant effect on the life of the parish.

Thus, well-thought-out strategy for film study in a local parish should provide for judicious selection of a few films each year according to a clearly defined purpose or goal, and that will determine their choice and how often this medium is used.

4. The Goals of Film Utilization

It is important that goals be clearly defined, since they must inevitably condition the approach and style of use. Though there may be many variations and combinations of specific goals in a parish, I should like to distinguish what I believe to be the four most basic possibilities. These are to assist in developing

1. Discernment regarding the positive and negative aspects of cultural input through the mass media.

2. Meaningful interpersonal relationships in which beliefs and values may be discussed in a climate of understanding and mutual Christian support.

3. Individual growth in relation to current personal, social, moral, and religious issues and problems.

4. Appreciation and understanding of the language of film.

It will be immediately obvious to the reader that these goals are not discrete or mutually exclusive. In every one some element of the others will also be found, but in any style of approach, one will always be dominant. In some parishes the use of secular films may be so varied that each of the four can receive major attention, while in others one or another will tend to predominate. All are valid. All are interrelated. This can be illustrated with a simple diagram.

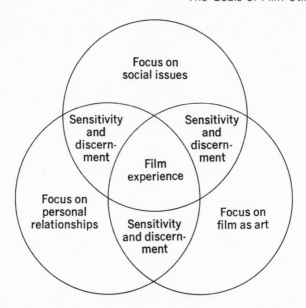

Regardless of which emphasis one chooses for the orientation of a particular film program in the parish, it will deal in some measure with each of the others. The style of use will be conditioned by the dominant goal or purpose selected. Only those in the actual situation can ultimately determine which is best for their parish.

5. SO HOW DO YOU DO IT ?

It remains now to present a brief description of what happens in a dialogical film study session, assuming that all have seen the film, that adequate time has been set aside (1 hour minimum), and that the group has been kept small enough to insure involvement on the part of all, or split up into several groups. No one pattern is best for all situations, but generally there should be an effort to

1. Recall the film, sharing what was seen and heard by all the participants.

2. Identify the issue or issues to which it speaks.

3. Relate what the film said on current issues, problems, etc., to the personal experience of the participants.

4. Compare or contrast what the film said with Christian beliefs and values as understood by the participants;

5. Share knowledge, insights, or feelings about the issues or problems discussed and understand each other's viewpoint or feelings.

Since these efforts will need direction, someone must act as leader, either by prearrangement or after the group has gathered in a comfortable place such as a private home, restaurant, or church meeting room. This is not a role of teacher or expert or final authority, but of enabler. His (or her) task is to see that dialogue takes place. A good leader will

Try to get each person into the discussion as soon as possible. There is a direct relationship between the length of time a person sits in a group without speaking and the difficulty of getting him to speak at all—for this reason the size of a discussion group should generally be limited to no more than 8 persons.

Not give speeches or be an answer man—a loquacious leader is a dialogue destroyer.

Raise significant questions.

Encourage the free expression of ideas, feelings, attitudes.

Maintain an uncritical attitude regarding the comments of others.

Avoid judgmental or prejudicial statements.

And the participants in the group also have responsibilities toward all others in the group. A good participant will

Share his insights, ideas, and observations freely.

Avoid monopolizing the conversation.

Uphold minority viewpoints.

Remember that "ideas have people" and that ridiculing ideas hurts people.

Help others in expressing their ideas, seeking to draw them out.

Acknowledge and honor different or opposing viewpoints.

Be willing to disagree and yet accept others without judgment.

Getting Started

Sometimes there will need to be little priming to get the dialogue going. Usually it is well for the leader to provide an opportunity for the group to *recall the film*. To do this it is helpful to ask a question which will enable each participant to give his own answer in his own way. Questions which help to do this might take the following pattern:

How would you describe to another person what the film is about?

Which scene, situation, or comment do you recall most vividly?

What scene, situation, or comment made you most angry or happy or sad, etc.?

With which person(s) or situations did you feel most akin?

What feelings experienced during the film do you recall most vividly?

Such questions, answered by each participant (perhaps all can respond to the same question), will reconstruct most of the film in their minds and get each one to speak as soon as possible. These shared feelings and experiences also become a part of the data input to the discussion.

The second need is to *focus the film*. Here there are two considerations that must be dealt with. The first relates to the film and the second to the viewers. To focus the viewpoint of the film, it will help to ask such questions as:

What do you think the central message of the film is?

What do you think the film is trying to communicate?

What statement does the film make about
<u>(General subject area)</u> ?

The second aspect of putting the film in focus requires that the participants be encouraged to react to the film in terms of their own perception of the issue(s), their own beliefs and values, their own feelings. To get at this, the leader or someone else present might ask a direct question of one or more of the group calling for a personal statement about where they stand in regard to the viewpoint of the film, and follow with questions which will enable the participant to further develop his thinking.

From this point on, the discussion may go in any direction. The best and most helpful agenda at any time or place is the one that develops in the group itself. There is no reason why all or even many aspects of a film must be dealt with to have a profitable experience.

Sometimes a discussion may be so fruitful that the group would like to continue it at another time. If this is the case, the following suggestions may be helpful. The group should

1. Decide together which issues raised by the film are to be discussed at subsequent meetings.

2. Make a list of these issues and some possible resources (magazines, books, articles, speeches, TV programs, other films, etc.) that will aid in such a discussion.

3. Decide on the next meeting time and place and what each one should do in preparation.

A Word about Questions

Sometimes little priming will be needed to get the dialogue going. But questions will inevitably be put and answers attempted as it progresses. It is important that questions be phrased so as to facilitate rather than close down conversation. Such inquiries do not ask for Yes or No or right or wrong answers, but for reactions and feelings. They deal with individual perceptions and have neither right nor wrong status, but give voice to personal interpretations. These elicited answers are unassailable because they are *facts*—another participant's interpretation from his point of view. Others may question them, but they must be honored for what they are.

At the close of this chapter are some study guides developed by the author for the Dialogue Thrust in Films for the Division of Parish Education of the American Lutheran Church. Their careful perusal will provide many insights into the kinds of question appropriate in a dialogue film study session.

It has been the experience of those involved in the type of film study advocated here that seldom will such a study end without the strong presence of the witness of the Scriptures. When Christians discuss the meaningful questions of their own life situations with others, the door is open for the Spirit of God to enter and do his revealing work. For as Jesus said, "Where two or three are gathered together in my name, there am I in their midst." Many have not only found their faith taking on new vitality through such encounters in secular film discussions, but have been driven back into the Scriptures for deeper and broader study. In some congregations the use of secular films in adult and youth education programs has been a spark that ignited whole new efforts to know more about the will of God for our time, while others have found for the first time a close and meaningful fellowship that awakened them to new and deeper experience of what it means to belong to the healing fellowship of the church.

To illustrate the principles discussed above I have selected the following material* from three study guides for inclusion here. Each represents a different type of film story and emphasis. *Cromwell* is an historical film dealing with large questions related to men and movements, political issues and forces, philosophy and theology. *The Learning Tree* deals laregly with current social issues. *I Never Sang for My Father* is a very personal film which probes into personal relationships and problems. It should be obvious, as I remarked earlier, that the nature of a film will to some extent dictate the type of approach and questions most appropriate in each case. In the following pages, note especially the emphasis on personal feelings and reactions, on introspection, on comparison and evaluation, and on personal decision. Note also in each case the effort to provide background and focus the film in the group consciousness.

*This material is quoted from study guides prepared for the Dialogue Thrust in Films of the Division of Parish Education, The American Lutheran Church, and published by Augsburg Publishing House. The full study guides are available from the Augsburg Publishing House, 426 South Fifth Street, Minneapolis, Minnesota 55415.

CROMWELL,
a Columbia Pictures Release

About the Film

   CROMWELL records the tumultous events that changed the English nation. It is told in terms of the two main protagonists of the English Civil War—Oliver Cromwell and King Charles I. As portrayed by Richard Harris and Alec Guinness, these two towering historical figures are neither heroes nor villains. Instead we see two men, each convinced of the righteousness of his cause and of God's approval and support, dragged deeper and deeper into the web of forces and events until one loses his head, the other his soul. Both were overwhelmed by the chain of events they had set in motion and destroyed by the impersonal and unrelenting force of history.

Who was right? Who was wrong? The film makes no attempt at an answer. It unfolds before us the men and events and leaves us to ponder the question: Who, in the long run, is master of his fate?

The film presents strong parallels to contemporary times. Here the question that seems to beg for an answer is: What is it in men, acting with all sincerity in what they believe are the best interests of their countrymen, that leads them to kill, plunder, and destroy the very people to whom they set out to give a better life? Why do the lives of the committed so often end violently, and at what point do we lose control over our actions and see them take control of us?

Oliver Cromwell (Richard Harris), Puritan, landowner, member of Parliament, sick at heart because of the conditions in the country he loves, vows to fight King Charles' flagrant disregard of justice and also the restoration of Catholic ritual to the Anglican service.

Charles I (Alec Guinness), a weak and vacillating king, is urged on by the queen (Dorothy Tutin) and Lord Strafford (Patrick Wymark) to disregard Parliament and take the money he needs for his wars. The battle is joined when Parliament refuses the king his money and forces him to sign the death warrant of Strafford. Cromwell accuses the king of treason and rallies the House to declare war against him.

The ragged forces of Parliament are beaten by the royal army at the Battle of Edgehill, and not until Cromwell raises and trains a new military force are the Parliamentarians able to defeat Charles and bring him back to London to stand trial for treason. Before the members of both Houses and the citizens of London Charles refuses to defend himself, claiming that Parliament has not the authority to try its king. His dignity and demeanor split his enemies, and Cromwell literally has to force the committee to sign the king's death warrant.

In 1649 Charles I is executed before a mob, and England is declared a republic. But Cromwell's dream of a just, truly democratic England is destroyed when Parliament is as arbitrary in its rule as the king was in his. Old and tired, Cromwell returns to London, and like Charles before him dissolves Parliament and declares his dictatorship, a burden he never wanted.

How to View a Historical Film

Cromwell is a historical film. This means, first of all, that certain objective facts such as names, places, and the dates of events as a part of technical history are being reported upon. *Cromwell* deals with events which transpired around and during the English Civil War of 1642-49. Second, however, as history it is an *interpretation* of persons and events, and reflects the bias of the script writer, director, and to some extent the producer and actors. But this is always the way with history; those who report

it say what they see and how they feel about it, with the eyes and understanding of their own experience. All history apart from the bare bones of verifiable dates, names, places, etc., is interpretation of human experience.

About the past events chosen for portrayal the question must be asked: Why were these particular incidents singled out for public notice? One answer may be: because they are seen by someone as comment or interpretation of our own present experience. Thus the historical film provides a unique opportunity to probe vicariously our own present experience for meaning, insight, and judgment, and hopefully to gain some guidance. *Cromwell* gives us an opening not only into the past but deeply into the present. It may possess the character of prophecy. The question of *meaning* for our own time always confronts us, and it is this question that should characterize our discussion of the film.

Men and Causes

Cromwell is basically the story of two men deeply dedicated to noble causes. What were these causes?

How were they similar or different?
What are their parallels in America today?
Who today would side with Charles I and the Royalists?
Who would be the counterparts of Cromwell and the Parliamentary forces?

Both Charles I and Oliver Cromwell believed they were acting in accord with the divine will.

What was the basis of confidence of each as to the righteousness of his acts?
Are these bases appropriate for identifying the will of God in our time and in our lives? Why, or when?

How did you feel about the involvement of the Protestant and Anglican clergy in the battle at Naseby? What parallels do you see in our present military involvement or arrangements?

Man and History

Cromwell enables us to view a series of large events and their effect upon individuals. The experience raises some questions for us about the meaning and force of history. To what extent was the course of the English Civil War the result of the will and force and conviction of the major characters? Did they determine the events, or were they determined by the events?

Recall the opening scenes of the film and Oliver Cromwell's intention to leave England.

Recall Cromwell's early speech in Parliament about the invasion and confiscation of common lands, and his later speeches when he confiscated by force the rights of the Royalists.

Do you feel Cromwell was really a cryptodictator in his early days, or did history change his views and conduct so drastically as to make him a dictator against his own will?

Who is really master of his own fate, according to the thrust of the film?

Account for Cromwell's evolution from a disillusioned and frustrated man about to flee his native land to a military man of war and political dictator. Trace the steps in his development and discuss the ethical basis for his major decisions.

It has been said that "power corrupts and absolute power corrupts absolutely." Was it *power* itself that finally captured Cromwell, or did his principle of individual freedom lead him to his position as Lord Protector of England?

As a virtual dictator, Cromwell launched England on one of its most prosperous periods. In view of the benefits he brought to England and the cause of constitutional government, do you feel the following is a valid appraisal of cause and effect?

I shall give this nation its self-respect. We will walk in this world with our heads high. I will liberate men's souls from the darkness of ignorance. I will build schools and universities. This will become the golden age of learning. I will bring the law within the reach of every common man. There will be bread and work for all. This nation will prosper because we are a godly nation and we do walk hand-in-hand with the Lord.

Obedience and Disobedience

Recall Cromwell's defiance of the king's commands, his demonstrations of disrespect for authority by remaining seated in the presence of the king. How would you compare his acts to many taking place today, when individuals

—desecrate church buildings?

—show contempt for duly constituted authority?

—disrupt worship services?

—hold sit-ins in public buildings and sanctuaries?

—refuse to submit to police authority and to college and university administrations?

Do you feel that Cromwell was right or wrong when he said his own mutinous troops "had no right to preach revolt and mutiny"? How did their actions and his own differ?

When John Pym and General Ireton pleaded for Cromwell's return to Parliament and to the king's war with Scotland, he replied, "Let Charles have his war with Scotland, 'tis no concern of mine."

Is such a refusal ever justified? When? On what grounds?

How did Cromwell's situation differ from that of today's draft card burner or conscientious objector? What of history's other revolutionaries?

When Parliament did not go his way, Cromwell declared that it did not represent the will of the people. Who determines the will of the people? How is it determined in our own nation?

The use of force to bring about social reform in England was a successful enterprise. Is this use of force justified?

What about force through demonstrations?
What about the Black Panthers and the SDS?
What about legal political force as over against civil disobedience and lawlessness?

How do you interpret Cromwell's pleas for individual freedom and self-government, when he blamed the Catholics for England's troubles and advocated their extermination? Is religious prejudice any better or different from social or racial prejudice?

King Charles said, "Democracy, Mr. Cromwell, is a foolish drollery based upon the notion that there are extraordinary possibilities in ordinary people." Abraham Lincoln talked of a government "of the people, by the people, and for the people." Which view does our current experience tend to support?

To what extent does our experience with inefficiency and corruption in high places, the disregard for minority groups, etc.

parallel the experience of England before Cromwell became Lord Protector?

Cromwell at last concluded that without absolute authority there can be no government.

> Are any people really wise and good enough to govern themselves?

> Is chaos and anarchy the ultimate end of democracy?

> What in England's Civil War experience may provide guidance in our own time of revolution?

THE LEARNING TREE,
a Warner Brothers–Seven Arts Production

About the Story

The film story of *The Learning Tree* is based on the book by the same title written by Gordon Parks, famed *Life* magazine photographer, and published in 1963 by Harper & Row.

The story, which is Gordon Parks' own story, provides us with the opportunity of looking through the eyes of a black man into the experience of a black boy growing up in the free state of Kansas in the 1920s. The boy, Newt Winger, is the son of deeply religious, hard-working parents who look at life with a what-can-we-learn-from-this attitude. Newt, in the far from idyllic surroundings of Cherokee Flats with all its prejudices and racism, is urged by his mother not to yield to bitterness but to let the place be his learning tree.

And learn he does! In the Huck Finn–type experiences recounted in the film we watch Newt as he learns about sex from an older woman who seduces him. He learns about the beauty of nature from the country that surrounds him. He learns about death when the local sheriff guns down a frightened Negro gambler. He learns about fear when forced to help find the gambler's body

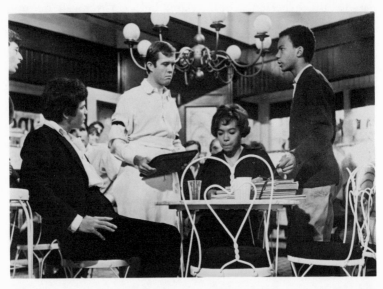

submerged in a river only a few feet from his favorite swimming
hole. He learns about love when a pretty new girl comes to town,
and about heartache when she goes away under clouded circumstances. He learns about pain when his mother dies all too sud-
denly and too soon. He learns about hate from a motherless
fifteen-year-old friend who virtually never had a chance. He
learns about immorality from a town honky-tonk "pleasure
house." He learns about honor and integrity when, all alone with
his conscience, he has to decide to save a white man's life at the
sacrifice of a black man's life.

Viewing the film is like looking at a series of snapshots strung
out in a row, each of which sweeps you into itself and bursts into
life, to give you the feeling of what it's like to be a black boy
growing up in a violent and racist society. The film is at times
melodramatic; this is due not to lack of artistry but to the fact that
life in the raw—life as it really is—is indeed often melodramatic
and unsophisticated. For sophistication is something acquired. It
can be a veneer with which a culture seeks to blur the harshness
and pain of human emotions and experience. Too frequently it

gets in the way of understanding what it really means to be a human being, and the problem of living as a human being in a dehumanizing society is what Gordon Parks deals with in his film.

The Learning Tree was selected as a United States entry in the twenty-third annual Edinburgh Film Festival scheduled at Edinburgh, Scotland, for the fall of 1969.

How to Begin

It is well to begin the discussion with a single question, to which each member of the group is asked to respond in his own way. One or more of the following may provide such a starting point:

How would you describe to another person what *The Learning Tree* is about?

What feelings experienced during the film do you recall most vividly?

With which person, situation, attitude, or idea in the film did you most identify?

Which scene do you recall most vividly?

Understanding the Film

1. Discuss the central concept of the film as indicated in its title, *The Learning Tree.* What were the lessons that Newt Winger learned in Cherokee Flats?

2. Where in the film did you see evil? Where did you see good? Discuss in light of the human inclination to characterize people as either good guys or bad guys. In what ways were they good or bad? What might this indicate about your concept of the nature of good and evil?

3. What varying views of life were presented in the film? With which do you most closely identify?

4. Where in the film was the center of hope?

5. What stereotypes did the film explode? What might this say about stereotypes in general?

6. Which people in the film responded in unexpected ways?

7. Which of your own beliefs and values were supported or refuted by the film?

8. Where did you see beauty in the film? Where did you see ugliness? Share and discuss your perceptions.

9. Recall Newt's words beside his mother's coffin: "I ain't afraid, Mama. I ain't afraid anymore." Why was he no longer afraid? What had he learned, and how had he learned it?

Discrimination and Prejudice

1. "Yep, boy, it's so. And you know what, Newt? I think sometimes if all the people in the world were made up of colors instead of just black and white it would be a happier world. A world all mixed up with wonderful colored people, nobody bein' the same as anybody else." Do you think the problem between the races is really color? Would the fanciful solution suggested by Uncle Rob change anything?

2. "Newt—I've been blind over thirty years. I can't see what color people are anymore. So when somebody does something bad or good, I don't figger his color into it. I only figger his deed." What is your reaction to Uncle Rob's words?

3. Recall the scenes of Marcus in prison and Newt in the school principal's office. Try to reenact these scenes. Express and discuss your feelings as you played the roles.

4. Discuss your reaction to the comments of Mr. Hall, the school principal, when Newt was taken to him by Miss McClintock.

5. Recall the treatment of Marcus in the town jail. Recast the scenes in terms of people and circumstances in your own community. What are the similarities or differences? What might you do about them?

6. Discuss the attitudes and actions of Law Officer Kirky over

against charges of police brutality in your own community. What progress have we made since the 1920s?

7. What were the problems Newt faced in trying to live up to his family's ideals and values? Is the problem any more acute for blacks than for whites in our society?

8. Compare the relationship of blacks and whites in the free state of Kansas in the 1920s to the same relationships in your community today. Discuss similarities and differences in terms of cause and effect.

9. Recall and list as many evidences of institutional racism in the film as you can. Compare with your community, naming situations, persons, etc.

10. Where in the film did you see evidences of a double standard regarding law and order? Compare to your community. What can you do about it?

11. Recall Miss McClintock's remarks to Newt about his future. How do you react to her advice? Why?

12. "I can make it on my own," Newt said to Kirky in the closing scene of the film. What might the attitude expressed here say about the realities faced in our black/white world?

Violence and Nonviolence

1. Where in the film did you see violence? Who used it? To what end? In what way is the violence of those seeking to obtain human justice any better or worse or different from violence used by segments of society to preserve their own privileges at the expense of others?

2. What encouragement does the film give to persons confronted with the choice of violence or nonviolence as ways of dealing with the problems that lead to racial tension in our society?

3. What do you think the film is trying to say about how the problem of racial justice can be solved?

4. On the basis of what it was like in Cherokee Flats in the

1920s, identify and discuss the handicaps faced by the disadvantaged in obtaining basic human rights. What can be done to remove them?

Society, Church—Beliefs and Values

1. Think of Marcus, the boy who seemed to have too much trouble. What factors in his world contributed to his problems and behavior? What might you (your church, group, family, etc.) do to help change similar factors in the lives of people in your community?

2. Are some lives unsalvageable in our kind of world? Why, or why not?

3. Compare and discuss the home life of Newt Winger and Marcus. What might this say about the importance of the home in the development of character and moral judgment?

4. What can this film teach us about the value of religious training in the home?

5. What does the film say about environment in relation to human behavior?

6. Chappie, the owner of the town brothel, said to Marcus: "Don't ask questions. Just do as you're told." To what extent is this good or bad advice in our world? What does obedience to such advice say about the person who follows it? Is there any alternative?

7. Recall the judge's speech to the crowd in the courtroom, regarding law and justice. He said to the crowd, "You pulled the trigger . . . you decided that he killed a white man, so you judged him . . . and executed him." Discuss the meaning of these words in the light of recent events such as the assassinations of John and Robert Kennedy, Martin Luther King, Jr., etc.

8. Mr. Hall said to Newt: "You owe Miss McClintock the highest respect." Do you agree or disagree? What is the basis of respect? How should you regard or deal with a Miss McClintock?

9. Which person in the film seemed to be the transmitter of

beliefs and values? Is this generally true in our culture? What can be done about it?

Understanding the Language of Film

Symbols are a form of communication shorthand by which we try to convey ideas, beliefs, values, and feelings. They are especially useful to the artist, who must convey his meaning in a limited time or space. In motion pictures, symbols in the form of objects or acts are abundantly used to say things that cannot be said as economically or eloquently through words.

As an exercise in understanding film language, it may be useful to share with others in your group the meaning of symbols you observed in the film. For instance:

How about the emphasis on eyes and seeing (recall Uncle Rob's blindness, the dark glasses, the dramatic shot of the animal's eyes, etc.).

In the context of the film what was the symbolic meaning of Newt's lying down beside his mother's coffin?

What about the way in which the shootings of Tuck and Marcus were filmed?

What other symbols did you observe?

I NEVER SANG FOR MY FATHER
a Columbia Pictures Release

About the Film

"Death ends a life! But it does not end a relationship which struggles on in the survivor's mind toward some resolution which it may never find."

These words of Gene Harrison's at the close of the film express a truth which must inevitably be faced by every human being. We can never escape the fact that we are the children of someone, and that somehow for better or for worse this relationship conditions us, calls for response, and is one link in a long chain of relationships.

Robert Anderson's screenplay tells the story of a man's relationship to his father, a relationship having but fleeting moments of splendor. On the surface and to the outsider the relation of these two men might seem most admirable; but inside, through the miracle of film we see what is there, we become aware of the heartache, the tension, and the frustration that robs the relationship of its potentially strengthening power. The film gives us an opportunity to know and weigh many of the serious questions that face us regarding the nature of our responsibility for those who bore and nurtured us to adulthood. These questions are raised with new perspective and force by our changing forms of modern life.

I Never Sang For My Father was produced and driected for Columbia Pictures by Gilbert Cates. The story was written for the stage and later adapted for the screen by Robert Anderson (*The Nun's Story* and *The Sand Pebbles*). It has been hailed by Judith Crist, dean of motion picture critics, as a "perfect film." Discussion and study groups will find it an excellent film on the subject of social and personal implications of human relationships. It is at once so personal and so universal that seeing it is to see oneself —past, present, and future.

Synopsis of the Film

A forty-year-old widower, Gene Garrison (Gene Hackman), on sabbatical leave from the university where he teaches, is torn between his responsibility to his parents and to himself.

His mother (Dorothy Stickney) still fawns over him, but he seeks the love of his father, Tom Garrison (Melvyn Douglas), which has always been denied him. Though Gene extends himself on their behalf, he inwardly resents their dependency.

His sister Alice (Estelle Parsons), banished by their father when she married a Jew, has moved to Chicago with her husband and raised a family there. She readjusted her way of life with the help of a psychiatrist. She emerges independent and very rational.

The mother is quite ill and subsequently dies. That his father doesn't show adequate sorrow over the loss angers Gene. When his sister comes east for the funeral, they conclude that a decision has to be made regarding their father's future.

Gene tries to establish a warmer relationship between his father and himself. His sister advises him to marry Dr. Peggy Thayer, a pretty divorcee he has met during a trip to California. She also cautions him not to sacrifice his life and future happiness to cater to an old man who will always treat him with disdain and never show him any real love.

They discuss getting a full-time housekeeper for their father, who is adamant about not wanting one. They even consider placement in a home for the aged, but this idea is soon discarded.

Highly emotional scenes erupt between all three. Gene decides to ignore Alice's advice and stay with his father temporarily.

During an unusual moment of warm, sensitive dialogue, the father reminisces and Gene hangs on to each word. He invites his father to move to California with him and his intended bride. Tom Garrison rejects the offer and virtually demands that they rather move east to live in his house with him. He angrily denouces Gene as an ingrate. Gene storms from the house with his fiancee, who has come east for a medical convention.

Though the break between father and son is never healed, they do subsequently and on rare occasions see each other. One day Tom Garrison is found seemingly asleep, but in fact dead, in front of his television set, as a shoot-'em-up Western proceeds before him. The differences between father and son have never been resolved—the sought-for relationship was never realized.

Dealing with Modern Films

Many feel the increasing trend toward frankness in film-making has passed the bounds of decency and good taste. Whereas numerous films are tasteless and often offensive to the discerning, frankness must not be regarded as always objectionable. Needless to say, while crude language, profanity, and four-letter words are never to be regarded as cultural gains, they are an undeniable part of human experience. In a modern realistic film the viewer should remember that he is being provided with a slice of life, not storybook experience. It tries to present life as it is really lived in these situations and by the people portrayed in the film. Words and actions contrary to the standards and tastes of the viewer are not, by their inclusion in the picutre, being advocated or approved for emulation. They are simply a part of the data to be read into the total filmic experience, and should not be allowed to divert the viewer from perceiving the real and deeper message of the film.

Opening Up the Film

Though they may be sitting side by side, no two people see the same film. Each person brings a context for what is on the screen. There are therefore, no right or wrong answers as to what a film is about. It is about whatever a person says it is. This does not mean that there will not be common elements in the feelings and interpretations of the several people in a discussion group. However, each person will also be a resource for enlarging and shaping the insight of others. In order to open up the film and involve the whole group in meaningful discussion, use the more appropriate of the two approaches offered.

1. Ask each participant to describe in one word the way the film made him feel. After going around the group with this question, circle it again asking each to describe the situations, statements, etc., responsible for their feelings.

2. Circle the group with one or more of the following questions, each time having all persons respond to the same question.

What significance do you see in the title of the film?

Which situation, scene, statement, or object do you recall most vividly?

Which person in the film was most like someone in your own experience? Who, and why?

What do you think the central message of the film really is?

These questions will help the group refocus the entire film. The discussion should be allowed to take whatever direction seems most meaningful to those involved. Use the following questions to help the group probe the experience to gain new insight and open new areas of concern.

Personal Roles

In terms of strengths, weaknesses, etc.,

1. How do you feel about Tom Garrison as a father?

2. . . . About Gene Garrison as a son?

3. . . . About Alice as a daughter?

4. What was the role of Margaret (Mrs. Garrison) in the family?

Family and Personal Relationships

1. What desirable qualities did you observe in the relationships of the members of the Garrison family? In what ways was it a good family?

2. What was undesirable about their relationships?

3. What clues does the film provide for ways in which family life can be strengthened?

4. Recall the kitchen scene when Alice tries to persuade Gene not to allow his father to dominate him. Was her appraisal of the situation right? Why?

5. If you were Gene and confronted with the situation after his father's death, how would you respond? Why?

6. Do you think Gene was justified in walking out on his father? Why, or why not?

7. How would you have wanted Gene to respond to his father's demands?

8. How (or when) might the father-son relationship have been strengthened?

9. What was it that made Tom Garrison a "remarkable man"?

10. What clues did the film provide to Tom Garrison's character?

11. At what point was Gene most open to loving his father? Why? What might this say to us about what helps or hinders personal relationships?

12. What does the statement, "Death ends a life but not a relationship," say about life's priorities?

13. If you could have been a friend to Tom Garrison, what might you have done to try to change him? Or do you feel no change was necessary—or possible?

14. What was the driving force in Tom Garrison's life? Discuss its effects on the family.

Family Responsibilities

1. What does a parent owe a child? Discuss this question in reference to Tom Garrison's attitude.

2. What does a child owe a parent? (Recall Alice's advice to Gene.)

Social Concern

Groups or individuals desiring to deal with social concerns related to the aging may explore questions such as:

1. Discuss your reactions to the scenes in which Gene visited the homes for the aged.

2. Recall the doctor's statement, "This is the other side of

our miracle drugs." Discuss the ethics of prolonging life past the point of usefulness.

3. It has been said that "people prepare for retirement but not for old age." What might we do to prepare ourselves more adequately for old age? How might we help parents, relatives, or friends prepare for old age?

4. Is it appropriate for parents (like Tom Garrison) to expect their children to shape their lives according to the physical and emotional needs of the parents? Why, or why not?

5. Who is really responsible for the care of the aged? Compare the attitudes of Gene and Alice.

6. What can children and friends do for the aged that retirement homes and pensions can never do?

7. What was the nature of Tom Garrison's need that impelled him to want his son to stay near him?

8. Discuss the pros and cons of living with one's family or of living in a reitrement home for the aged.

9. Ought children to feel guilty about living their own lives apart from their aging parents?

6. SOME THINGS TO KEEP IN MIND

The use of secular films in the church's service is not really as mysterious or difficult as might at first appear. The whole matter revolves around two activities: seeing films and discussing them. Both raise the same basic questions as to where, when, how, and by whom. Since this is what film utilization as here perceived is all about, to these questions we shall address ourselves now.

Where

Secular films to be used must be seen. This means that effort must be exerted to get people to see them, and preferably at the local theater. While not opposed to screening secular films on church premises, I do not intend to discuss that option here. Others have already done so very effectively for us.* Those of us who have worked in this area want to stress the seeing of secular films in their natural setting—that is, the local theater. We believe this is very important for several reasons.

First, it is the setting in which these films are made to be shown, and the equipment and facilities there are much more conducive to filmic experience of quality. Most feature films run for nearly

*William G. Jones, *Sunday Night at the Movies* (Richmond, Va.: John Knox Pres., 1967).

two hours. To sit that long in a church pew or on a folding chair in the parish hall is very difficult for most people, and robs the experience of the kind of total involvement possible when one is more comfortable. Also, 16mm. projection equipment under the conditions that usually prevail with portable equipment is visually and aurally inferior to the kind of audio-visual control possible with a professional 35mm. theatrical setup. All this cheats the experience of the kind of depth involvement for which secular films are made.

Second, something happens to the nature of the experience when a film is shown on church premises. People appear to think and react differently on the church's "turf" than on the world's "turf." Their response to a film, in my experience, is totally different when it is seen in a theater from what it is when seen in the church building. Perhaps this is because of the conditioning of our minds that has taken place over the years in our relation to the church. Whatever the reason, people respond more honestly and freely both during and after seeing a film in the local theater. From the viewpoint of the quality of the total filmic experience, secular films are best seen in the theater.

When

Also (and related to the *when*), the fact is obvious that one advantage of using secular film is that it is on the world's agenda. Many people are already seeing current offerings in the local theater. This is when the film is news and a part of the cultural wash. Its impact on the culture is usually greatest during its first run, and there is more motivation for people to see a given film when friends, neighbors, and children are seeing and talking about it, and newspapers, billboards, magazines, radio, and TV are publicizing it.

How We See Films

It is clear that before one can fully understand a language he must know something about its structure. True, people do learn to speak before they learn rules of grammar; nonetheless, the better one understands the grammatical structure of language, the greater the possibility for meaningful communication. Today people are conditioned to act and react to the film medium and its electronic counterpart, the television image. Though different processes are involved in the presentation of motion pictures on television (the one being electronic impulses and the other a film print), the result, "moving" pictures, has the same impact on the viewer. He may not understand and generally cannot articulate why he feels as he does in viewing a film or a television program. Though he may not need to be a technical expert in either, it is important, especially in this visual age, that he understand some of the "grammar" of film language.

It is appropriate, therefore, for a local parish to provide some specific help to its members in the language of film. This may be offered through workshops, clinics, or longer courses on film understanding and appreciation. The goal, of course, is to help people through understanding and appreciation of film to be better able to respond to and in their own culture—and to develop a more or less determinative, or at least conscious, participation in their own belief and value formation.

But important as it is for participants in any program using secular movies to have some acquaintance with the language of film, it is even more important that they have some understanding of the language of relationships and the principles of dialogue. Therefore any parish which takes seriously the use of secular films in its educational program will provide for such training through some courses on communication, including both principles and skills, especially for those who will serve as discussion leaders in the program. By applying the principles and practicing the skills in the film discussion groups, they will also provide a learning-by-doing training experience for other participants.

However this is done, its importance must be underscored. True dialogue does not take place automatically with the assembling of a group of talking people. It requires a mutual acceptance and practice of certain dialogical skills.

Who Sees Them

A study conducted in 1966–67 by the Motion Picture Association of America reported that four out of five of sixteen- to twenty-year-olds attend a motion picture once a month or more. Fifty-two percent of those from sixteen to twenty report that their attendance at motion picture theaters is increasing.* In 1970, the latest year for which figures are available 68 percent of all moviegoers were between the ages of sixteen and thirty-nine, while 43 percent of all moviegoers were between the ages of sixteen and twenty-four. Persons eighteen and over bought 74 percent of all theater tickets sold.** It was also discovered that education is a greater stimulus to moviegoing than is higher income. We are living in a time when more and more people are receiving better and better education. One might logically interpret this to mean that there will be an increase in the use of secular films in the future.

This indicates that the youth and young adult population are the most "cinemate." They attend films for various reasons, but they do attend, and this is significant. One commentator has noted that, for all the enthusiasm the younger generation has

*Figures from Susan Rice, "Theatrical Films are an Important Part of the Classroom Without Walls, *Media and Methods,* January 1969, pp. 56–57.

**Quigley, Martin Jr., ed. *International Motion Picture Almanac.* New York; Quigley Publications, 1972

shown for the "negative witness films" such as *Easy Rider, The Graduate, Mash,* and others, they are equally disposed to the more positive or purely entertainment films, such as *Mary Poppins, Lovebug, Love Story,* etc. I mention this simply to indicate that the younger generation may be easier to involve in the film study program, and will certainly better understand the church's use of secular films, than the older generation. This means that more energy, care, and ingenuity may be needed to involve the over-thirty generation, and that more work will have to be done in helping them appreciate what film is about as a medium than with those who have been raised on television.

7. THE PASTOR
AND SECULAR FILMS

Just as a pump may need priming before it will flow, so perhaps those who are not accustomed to thinking of secular films in their parish programs will appreciate some suggestions in order to start their own creative wells flowing. Therefore I dare to set down several pages concerning ways in which secular films are already being used by pastors in local parishes, and to make a few suggestions and observations about related matters.

Tell Them to Go

In most churches there is little hesitation in recommending the participation of parishioners in certain recreation or entertainment activities in the community. If one is near a major league ball park, very often a church day is planned, or the organizations arrange an outing to the ball park. Bowling, and golf tournaments, high school plays and activities, and other civic functions such as parades and celebrations are frequently announced in church services or publications as worthy of participation.

Why not encourage people to attend significant movies playing in the community? Some may argue that for the church to do this would be to endorse whatever kind of action or emphasis, language or thought pattern, the recommended film may present. Yet no one thinks that by urging its parishioners to participate the church is endorsing any of the unseemly language or activity that may take place at the ball park, bowling alley, or even a church picnic. Doubtless we have here a hangover in attitude from another generation, which regarded any association with or participation in the theater as inherently wicked. Such an attitude in this latter half of the twentieth century is difficult to understand, yet it does persist in varying degrees in many places. Suffice it to say that perhaps one of the best ways to begin the process of helping people understand the revolution that has taken place in theology in our time—which has all but erased the dividing line between the sacred and secular—is to diligently call significant movies to the attention of parishioners and urge their attendance. For this purpose oral announcements at church services and meetings, items in bulletins and parish papers, and posters on bulletin boards will all help. If we do not begin to acknowledge in direct and meaningful ways that God may be able to work through motion pictures and local theaters as well as in church buildings, we perpetuate the ancient myth of the bifurcated universe of sacred and secular and even make a mockery of the incarnation of God in the earthly human body of Jesus of Nazareth.

Speak about Them

Every pastor or teacher needs a continuing fresh supply of illustrations for his sermons and teaching. Yet how seldom (except to bemoan the sad state of morals in our time) do most pastors use the world of secular films as a source of rich and meaningful illustrations for biblical messages. These pastors either do not see movies or cannot make the connection between the Bible or theology and life as it is portrayed in the visual imagery of the screen. Instead of scouring dusty tomes for ancient, hackneyed,

and puerile illustrations for their sermons and other presentations, preaching ministers would do well to become acquainted
with current secular films and—occasionally at least—use illustrations from them in their speeches and sermons. It will inevitably strike a responsive chord in many of his listeners, for they too
will have been to the movies and will share that common experience as a basis for understanding.

If the preacher or speaker does use such material, he will do
so through a process of interpretation and application; and this
in itself may alert people to the power of film to speak to them
in their concerns and dilemmas. It will also place before them a
pattern of the way in which secular films can be interpreted and
applied to life. Certainly it is no credit to any person who seeks
to communicate with modern man to ignore completely or to
regard only negatively any of the forms through which modern
communication takes place.

Secular films are in themselves a message (totally apart from
their messages) to modern man. They can be a rich source of
illustrative material for those who attempt to communicate in
relevant and meaningful ways.

Films as Sermon Text and Context

Earlier I stated that many current secular films may be likened to
twentieth century equivalents to the parables of Jesus presenting
reality in a mythical form. The writer selects situations from
human experience to illuminate certain truths. The characters
are creations of the mind of the writer or author. They have being
only in terms of the reality portrayed in the move and in relation
to the truth being presented. But through them the viewer comes
into contact with the reality, the characters, and the situation they
were designed to illuminate.

It was the same with the parables of Jesus. He used simple
stories of common events and situations to reveal truth to those

who were open to his words. Most of these little tales were not
outwardly religious at all but had to do with property, relationships, and so on.

The stories he told in the form of parables make up a large
portion of the recorded teaching of Jesus. They have been told
for two thousand years and have become very familiar to all of
us. Because they are recorded in what we regard as Holy Scrip-
ture, we have endowed them with special significance, power, and
honor.

But think for a moment. If Jesus were here physically today to
carry out his redeeming ministry, where would he find the forms
through which to communicate with modern man? Since he did
use the most powerful and illuminating teaching devices available in his time, one feels he might often today speak his truth
in terms of secular films. Instead of sitting on the lake shore or
by the wayside drawing pictures with his words, he might well
invite his hearers into the secular theater with the invitation, "He
who has ears to hear, let him hear." Indeed, virtually all of Jesus'
parables can be paralleled in some secular film, different only as
to setting and detail, but unvarying in the truth they reveal.

It is in keeping with such an understanding of modern media
to see in some secular films the texts for sermons and to find in
them the means for God to speak His creative and redeeming
word to the alerted minds and feelings of His people. Secular film
may thus be a vital resource to proclaim God's truth from the
pulpit. Sermons can be built upon them in compelling and forceful ways.

An example of just such use is found in the preaching—using
a modern form of communication—of the Rev. Dennis Nyberg,
then pastor of Lake Harriet United Methodist Church in Minneapolis, Minnesota. * In the fall of 1968 he delivered a series of
sermons on the major events and periods marking our human

*Since June 1969 Mr. Nyberg has been pastor of the First United Methodist
Church in Palo Alto, Calif.

pilgrimage from birth through life. Based on then current secular films, they were entitled as follows:

> Birth—"What to Do about Rosemary's Baby"
> Youth—"The Graduate—into Whose World?"
> Marriage—"Who's Afraid?"
> Work—"Up the Down Staircase"
> Death—"The Swimmer Homeward"

The film used in each case is obvious. Each sermon explored the truth of the film as it relates to the Scriptures and the Christian faith and life. As to the result of this effort, Mr. Nyberg said, "They were received with phenomenal response and have given us a clue as to where meaningful myth-making for contemporary man is being achieved."

One could not participate in such a series of sermons without having something happen to his perception of the nature and meaning of film for our modern life. It seems clear that Mr. Nyberg and others who have made similar use of secular films have discovered a real clue to meaningful communication in our increasingly visual culture.

I am not advocating that such a procedure be followed every Sunday. However, if it could be done on occasion, when a significant film is available, or even a series of them—as Mr. Nyberg found, it would go a long way in helping people come to a new understanding of the film medium as it relates to us as Christians today.

The Secular Film as Sermon

In 1966 after seeing the film *A Patch of Blue*, a Lutheran minister was so moved he said he felt he had to run out of the theater and "find a blind girl to help." He said, "I've preached on and heard countless sermons about the Good Samaritan, but never have I been so inspired to put the parable to action as I was by the film *A Patch of Blue*." Commenting again later he said, "If that film were showing in my town at the time of my church service, I'd forget the offering for the day, lock the church doors and tell those who came to worship, 'The service is at the theater this morning.' "

Why not? If we really believe in a secular theology and that God can speak anywhere and through any means, why must we always launch our sermons from behind the secure fortress of the church's pulpit, in verbal form? The stained-glass windows of the sanctuary depicting biblical parables and incidents in the life of Christ had their original purpose in proclaiming the Gospel, but today their impact may be dwarfed by their parallels in modern dress in secular motion pictures.

If the approach suggested here seems extreme and too far out to win credence, one need only recall the incident of the rich young ruler with whom Jesus spoke. This young man came to him seeking spiritual direction, some guiding word. He was doubtless surprised that Jesus did not give that word immediately but directed him elsewhere. In effect he said to him, "Don't hang around here for what you're seeking. What you need to do is go and sell all your possessions, and in doing that you will discover what is necessary to following me and finding your salvation." The point was that through such an act the meaning of discipleship would be forcefully revealed to him. It was not only direct counsel of the truest sort, but also a teaching device, used by Jesus in order to make his point.

What would be the impact upon a congregation of such action as the enthusiastic pastor proposed with *A Patch of Blue*? Doubtless some would be highly offended. Many would be confused, others rejoice. But properly handled, it could make a powerful point about how God speaks to man in a variety of ways. If it could happen just once as the pastor imagined, what an interesting learning experience would take place!

For the fainthearted, perhaps a more modest approach would serve. Here are other possibilities of using the film as sermon.

Each assumes the presence of a suitable picture playing in the local theater within easy distance of the church.

The regular worship service takes place on Sunday morning, but instead of the usual sermon, the pastor announces that the sermon for the day will be presented at the local theater that afternoon or evening.* He would then use his usual sermon time to prepare the congregation for the filmic experience. Among other things, he should explain briefly the nature of communication through film. He would not tell what to look for in terms of message or morals, but rather how to view a film so that it will speak most forcefully and how to talk about it afterward with the family or a group of friends gathered for that purpose.

A prepared study guide of a film showing locally could be distributed as worshipers leave the church or as the offering is being received. Depending on how enterprising the pastor is, and how adequate the film, the sermon the following Sunday might deal with one or more issues from it. Or a dialogue sermon could take place, with certain laymen participating. Or there might be open discussion of the film, its message or meaning, led by the pastor and involving the whole congregation.

Another approach to secular film as sermon would move the worship service to the theater on a specific Sunday, and from Sunday morning to afternoon. Arrangements having been made in advance with the theater management, the congregation would be informed by advance notice that worship service on the set date would take place at the local theater. The time of the service could be set for thirty minutes before the first showing of the film. The pastor would conduct the worship service, including an offering for the purpose of paying admissions to the theater of those present. The service would

---

*If such a surprise might offend too many parishioners, some announcement of the event could be made the Sunday preceding.

conclude with the film as sermon, the worshipers being encouraged to talk about it afterward in their homes or in small groups at their own discretion.

The foregoing suggestions and examples are but a few of many that might have been presented. However, perhaps these few will indicate some of the exciting possibilities that secular films offer the pastor for a marquee ministry that can open the door to new effectiveness in his preaching and teaching.

8. HELPS FOR THE LEADER IN A FILM PROGRAM

If you are already well versed in film, skip this section and proceed immediately to explore other programmatic aspects of film use. However, if your interest in employment of secular film in the service of the church is just taking on life, it may help to read and act upon the information on the next few pages. Since rivers never rise higher than their sources, the leader in any church-wide effort to use secular films must become both cinemate and aware of the film scene.

Becoming "Cinemate"

The best way to learn to swim is to get into the water. The same principle applies to learning about film. Seeing a lot of films is an indispensable and continuing task of the film educator. The use of some good books on the subject will also heighten the value of the exposure and hasten one's development of expertise. I want to refer to three books (more are listed in the bibliography) which may give the novice a running start in dealing with films.

The first, though written for use in a high school film course, was designed to provide any reader with a quality of experience as nearly like that of viewing a film as is possible with a printed page. It is *Exploring the Film*, by William Kuhns and Robert Stanley. * Its fifteen brief, well-illustrated chapters provide a simple but adequate introduction to what film is all about, with special emphasis on the language of film. An excellent leader's guide has been prepared for those who, having read the book, want to teach it to others. The two volumes can be used effectively with both youth and adults in a parish program.

Another small but helpful book, widely used, covering much of the same material as the first but with greater emphasis on parish utilization, is *Sunday Night at the Movies*, by G. William Jones.** And one of the best presentations, with more depth on the art of film, is *The Film Experience: Elements of Motion Picture Art*, by Roy Huss and Norman Silverstein.†

Awareness—Keeping Tab

Next is the task of becoming and staying informed about what is happening in the world of secular films: what films are being made, being talked about, and being shown, where and when. Daily newspapers and national magazines carrying film reviews and comments are a ready resource for this.

Of special value are these additional periodicals: *Film Information*, a monthly publication of the Broadcasting and Film Commission of the National Council of Churches,‡ and *Catholic Film Newsletter*, published by the National Catholic Office for Motion Pictures.††

Both of these publications review films in current release. Both carry the code rating symbols of the Motion Picture Association (the *Newsletter* offers its own ratings also). Reviews in these two

*Dayton, Ohio: George A. Pflaum, 1968.
**Richmond, Va.: John Knox Press, 1967.
†New York: Dell Publishing Co. Delta Book, 1968.
‡Box 500, Manhattanville Station, New York, N.Y. 10027, $6 per year.
††Suite 4200, 405 Lexington Avenue, New York, N.Y. 10017, $6 per year.

periodicals, while not always agreeing with each other, do speak from a background of the Christian tradition.

While reading reviews is vital to film awareness, it should be remembered that they are written by individuals and invariably reflect the particular bias of the reviewer. One should therefore regularly read several reviews in both religious and secular publications. It will also be helpful if persons involved in film utilization occasionally try their own hand at writing reviews (though they are never published). This makes one more sensitive as to one's own judgment and standards regarding film, and more discerning regarding the reviews written by others.

A problem often encountered in reviews in secular publications is the very heavy emphasis on the artistic or technical aspects of the film. Many pictures which are regarded as poor on the basis of such evaluations, by other standards may prove very useful for the church's purpose.

Beware of Newspaper Ads

It goes without saying that newspaper, billboard, and magazine ads for films are a source for keeping up on the current film scene. But here a word of caution is in order.

Without a doubt the theater page is the worst page in any newspaper. Those who design the advertising copy for secular films are in many cases the film industry's own worst enemy. Many of the ads reveal an utter lack of understanding about the nature of film or of people, and indicate little faith in the ability of a good product to sell itself without the use of crude emphasis on sex and violence. Regardless of the subject matter of a film, the advertising usually focuses on sex or violence or both, often exaggerating these elements, and seldom revealing what the film is actually about. A case in point is the ad pictured on the opposite page. The impression given is that this is a film with heavy

and explicit emphasis on sex. Anyone who has seen it knows how distorted that implication is.

Also, it must be said that the rating code symbol in ads may be no accurate barometer as to the quality of a film, its subject matter, or in many cases its appropriateness for special audiences or age groups. Some X or R pictures are actually more appropriate and deserving of church attention than some labeled G or PG (see Chapter 2). This fact makes it all the more important for those who would make creative educational use of secular films to keep aware, and develop personal discernment and understanding of the current film scene.

Of Course You Could Take a Course

There are few educational institutions today of any significance which do not provide some kind of course in film and film appreciation. Colleges, universities, and evening high schools in all parts of the country offer dozens of workshops each year. For a clergyman today this may deserve as high a priority as attending an institute on the latest theological luminary or even a clinic on urban ministries. Film leaders should consider training in this area a necessity.

Most denominational offices of TV, radio, and films, and/or divisions of education, likewise offer workshops and materials on film. A few publish, semiregularly, materials for film study in the congregation. However, for the most part this has been left to independent agencies.

To know what opportunities for film study may be available in your immediate area, you may write the American Film Institute, 1815 H Street, N.W., Washington, D.C. 20006, requesting their listings of film study opportunities in institutions of both secondary and higher education. They also are a source of information about many workshops and seminars on film-making and appreciation throughout the country each year.

In conclusion, I want to stress that the need for religious leaders to become "cinemate" and aware of the current scene regarding secular films transcends their specific planned utilization. Any pastor or priest who does not know what films are playing locally and what, therefore, his people are seeing, is guilty of a serious omission in his effort to serve and understand them. He is also missing a great opportunity to tie into the lives of people at meaningful levels. The films people choose to see have much to say about their problems, fears, concerns, hang-ups, and human needs.

9. THE FILM FESTIVAL

More and more parishes are discovering new excitement in youth and adult education programs through the arrangement of film festivals in the local theaters. Current films, about which I have said most, bring with them contexts and opportunities for various types of use.

However, it is possible to *create* a context through special planning, by bringing back to the screen of the local theater good older films. Because of the specific context set up, the older films acquire new meaning. In most places there is an unrecognized willingness on the part of theater owners, managers, and film distributors to be of assistance to any congregation, school, group, or organization wanting to make special use of films.

Every movie theater has certain nights of the week which draw a very small audience and consequently little revenue. If the management can cover its operating expenses or even increase its revenues on those nights, it will make special arrangements for booking special films, and especially a group or series of films. Older pictures are more easily scheduled because the priorities established for first-run exhibition no longer apply. They can therefore be shown at reduced cost to the exhibitor whenever it fits into his program. In most cases, especially in moderate- to large-sized communities, theater managers will welcome this kind of opportunity to bring people into his theater.

A film festival can be arranged to last over a period of weeks, showing the selected pictures on one prearranged night each week. The films, chosen on the basis of a range of topics, may take up a new subject each time; or they can be selected on a common theme, so that individual films highlight a particular aspect of it.

There are many sources for choice of subject matter and films to set it forth. One excellent resource is *Screen Experience: An Approach to Film*, edited by Sharon Feyen,* which not only deals with the general background of films, but has a section on programming with listings appropriate for forty-seven different themes and approaches. Both Hollywood and foreign pictures are named and broken down into categories of documentary, western, mysteries, romances, musicals, comedies, and short films. Topics included are, for example: prejudice as it limits man; finding one's place in the world; men at war; individual conscience in an indifferent world; growing toward maturity; what really is truth, honor, virtue; an individual's fight for integrity; accent on the family; it's a women's world; ask any man; social problems. The films are described in terms of their message. This volume also has suggested supplementary reading material for each emphasis. The book is invaluable for those who want to use secular films in the service of the church.

Another source is the previously mentioned *Sunday Night at the Movies*. This, too, contains a helpful listing of available secular films grouped according to basic themes. Some of these are: confrontation by the truth; integrity versus expediency; justice and mercy; the meaning of death; racial prejudice; etc.

In addition to these two, there are many catalogs from various film companies and rental agencies, but these are generally less helpful because of their brevity and the lack of insight into religious or educational emphases.

If you are planning a film festival, either for your local parish

*Dayton, Ohio: George A. Pflaum, 1969.

or cooperatively in your community, the following suggestions will prove helpful.

1. Decide on the emphasis and schedule. (What are you really trying to do with the film festival and when can you do it best?)

2. Develop understanding of what films might be helpful. (The local theater manager may be cooperative but will generally tend to think primarily of typical religious categories, so be prepared with insights of your own as to films that might be used.)

3. Present the plan to the theater manager and discuss possibilities for its execution.

4. Plan with him for the best time and work out a calendar. (Allow 6–8 months for planning and preparation).

5. Decide together on fees, costs, advertising, etc.

6. Publicize and promote the program.

There are infinite possibilities for conducting the film festival, and each situation will be different. The following description may yield suggestions for your own situation.

The local Lutheran pastor in Montevideo, Minnesota, decided to conduct a film festival. He met first with the local theater manager and the regional manager of a chain of theaters in that area. After discussing his hopes and plans and some of the possibilities, they were able to work out the following arrangements together. They would show four different movies on Tuesday nights during February. For these they would offer season tickets, to be priced at $5, each ticket to admit two adults and two children. The theater would provide the tickets and the normal amount of advertising. The young people in the Couples' Club of the church were responsible for ticket sales. They were limited to the sale of three hundred tickets. The management agreed to provide the church with a cash gift of $250, if it sold over two-hundred tickets.

Reports from Harry Greene, vice-president of Midcontinent

Theater Corporation, indicated that the festival was a huge success, and he has encouraged many others to do the same kind of thing. This is an illustration of how the needs of both church and local theater were well met by teaming their energies. Perhaps it should be pointed out that the church should be willing to pay its own way in any such endeavors. The theater manager in providing the specially priced ticket and even a contribution to the church was exceedingly generous in the situation in Montevideo. Most theater managers or owners will be willing to grant special concessions on ticket prices, but they should not be expected to do so.

Above all, the promotion of a film festival, however worked out, should be for purposes of meaningful education and should not be approached as another way of making money. The goal must be clearly education and understanding through the use of film experiences. A film festival offers a fine opportunity to accomplish this goal.

10. THE LOCAL THEATER AS COMMUNITY FORUM

According to the International Motion Picture Almanac for 1971, there are 14,000 motion picture theaters operating in the United States (9,500 indoor and 4,500 outdoor theaters). They are within reach of approximately 90 percent of the population. Though most often thought of as entertainment facilities, they have other aspects that are significant in terms of the life and welfare of the local community and the church's concerns. They are also a part of the business community, the educational force, the social life, and the cultural climate of the total immediate area. In all these aspects, local theaters will either add to or detract from the well-being of the community. They can be forces for good or for evil, but their effect is seldom neutral.

I would like to discuss one use of the local theater that enables it to render a unique service for good. This is its employment as a community forum, a place where people may come together and share a common experience which can minister to the needs of the total area.

In every community, large or small, there are social concerns relating to its own life and well-being as well as to the nation and the world. One of the continuing needs in our culture is for neutral places for bringing people together to discuss and take action in regard to issues. I suggest that the local theater can be that place.

First of all, it is a public place. Anyone who has the price of admission regardless of race, color, creed, or political persuasion, is accustomed to feel free to enter. This means that it is neutral ground for all elements and age groups in a society. Second, it has a product which brings all kinds of people together and enables them to share a common experience. Though no two persons are likely to have exactly the same experience while viewing a film, they are nevertheless involved in its content together, at a specific time and place.

Now, if the film is one which deals in any way with a social, moral, religious, or political issue that affects the lives of these people, it may be used as a means of opening up the issue and the articulateness of those who see it for purposes of discussion, which hopefully may lead to some kind of inward decision-making and even action regarding that issue. The theater, therefore, has the potential of becoming a catalyst in a community forum on any given subject.

Social crises of our time have fostered large efforts to involve people in issue-centered dialogue. Some major efforts in this connection have been the development of town meetings, town talks, or faith-in-life institutes, as well as rural and urban crisis programs. These have been designed to make use of all the existing agencies and resources of a community. In these programs, the mass media have served a catalytic function, with secular films playing a significant role.

One example is a "Communi-action Conference on Ministry Skills for the 70's" held in Dubuque, Iowa in the fall of 1969. This was sponsored by Wartburg Theological Seminary on the basis of a grant from the National Crisis Fund of the American Lutheran Church. The focus was community-wide, and one vital part of the program was the inclusion of the then-current film *The Learning Tree,* described in Chapter 4. Special showings of the film were provided by the Grand Theater in Dubuque for persons attending the conference and other educational and religious leadership in the community. Following the screening of the film, discussion was held in the theater. The film provided a point of reference, but more than that, it succeeded in giving all those who saw it a common awareness of what it is like to be a black youth growing up in a white racist society. Thus a movie shown in the local theater established the context for a community forum. Many who took part in the conference regarded this experience as one of the high points of a very fruitful conference.

In such situations, current secular films can provide the means of centering discussion; in other circumstances older films brought back for a special showing have served the same end. The point is not which films are better for the purpose, but the fact that the local theater has a role in serving the area by providing both site and content for a community forum on critical issues.

Another illustration of a creative way in which a movie theater became the source of a community forum happened during Brotherhood Week in February, 1970 in the village of Minnetonka, Minnesota. A group known as the Excelsior Human Relations Commission sought a way to celebrate National Brotherhood Week. Having heard of *The Learning Tree,* it succeeded in arranging for a special screening in the local Tonka Theater on February 22, when the schools were dismissed for George Washington's Birthday. The film was shown at a matinee hour for the school children and others who could attend, not as a part of the regular playbill, but as an added offering.

The total program was arranged as follows. Working through the theater manager and Warner Brothers, permission was obtained to show the film in this special way. In the junior and senior high schools on the preceding Thursday and Friday, announcements were made over the PA system of the film showing and an invitation extended to all students to attend free of charge; on the Sunday preceding the occasion, also, churches were asked to announce it to their congregations and invite them to see the film. After the film showing, discussion was held in the theater regarding the black and white crisis in our time. During the following week teachers in history, social studies, and literature classes discussed the film further with students. Here again the theater was the means of a community forum, at least for the youth, on a critical social issue.

Stated below are what I believe to be the more significant values adding weight to the possibility of the local theater serving as catalyst for a community forum.

The local movie theater is a neutral place having no creed, viewpoint, or ideology to protect or foster. It is a community resource in the same way a public library is.

Through films the theater provides the community with a costly and powerful educational tool of great appeal.

The value of film as a wraparound culture gives the viewer the possibility of both involvement and detachment regarding its subject matter, and fosters greater objectivity.

The theater provides a variety of times—day and evening—when people may participate.

By comparison with speeches and reading, film and dialogue are more attractive to more people as a source of information on any subject.

Films have a great potential for conversational spillover and continuity.

Issues raised or dealt with in current films are frequently underscored in the public mind by discussion of the film in other media.

There are numerous creative ways in which local theaters can use secular films to foster community discussion. The few specific suggestions given here may be used and enlarged upon or varied to meet local needs.

Discussion in the Theater

The most obvious and direct arrangement is to have discussion in the theater immediately after showing the film. The basic format is, following the final credits, to turn up the house lights and have a panel of three or four persons appear on the stage to raise —or speak to—specific issues or problems presented in the movie. After a few minutes of comment by the panel, questions or comments from the audience may be invited.

Panel discussion and audience participation in the theater following the film.

The use of some device such as a panel to bring the audience out of the silence and internal thought processes imposed by the viewing experience is very necessary. People do not immediately or easily move from the viewer/participant to a talking/participant role. This is especially true if the film has dealt with beliefs and values and involved the viewer at a deep emotional level. Film discussion is primarily a cognitive process, while viewing is primarily an affective process. One's emotions must be subjected to rational control before discussion is possible. The use of a panel to speak briefly about the film sets up a bridge between the highly affective and internal experience of the viewer and the more cognitive and rational process of discussing it. The anticipated intensity of the viewer's emotional involvement in the film should be carefully considered in planning the procedure used.

Necessary to such use of the theater for discussion purposes is the availability of microphones and amplifiers. Provision for both platform mikes for the panel and mikes for the audience should be made. One mike in each aisle should be sufficient. If the local theater is not equipped with mike jacks into the main sound system, auxiliary or portable amplifiers will have to be provided for the occasion. Since hearing and speaking are essential to film discussion, no attempt to use a local theater for discussion should be made without adequate provision for sound amplification.

The amount of time devoted to talk in the theater will be subject to the arrangement for the screening. If for instance discussion is to take place during the regular screening schedule, it will not be possible to prolong it. The maximum time a theater could allow for such a program would probably not exceed half an hour. However, even in that short a time, careful planning and a good moderator can make valuable exchange possible. If the film is being shown at a special screening outside the hours of normal operation (that is, in the morning or afternoon in most local theaters), the time for discussion can be expanded to an hour or more. In this case one might involve the audience in conversations where they sit by asking people in alternate rows to turn around and, facing the persons behind them, work in groups of four or six to discuss their own questions or observations or those suggested by the moderator or panel. This should be followed by open question-and-answer time between the panel or moderator and the audience.

One of the primary advantages of this technique is to stimulate and focus discussion in the wider community on the issues involved. In an opportunity of this sort, the ideas and reactions of people of varying religious, political, ethnic, and social backgrounds may be aired.

Usually such an occasion will be a part of a larger, more comprehensive effort in the community. Perhaps the very fact that the theater is used in an educational context will have a positive effect on the public's image of the movie theater as an educative force.

The program might involve the local newspaper, in special effort to encourage people to carry on the discussion in letters to the editor. An alert theater manager should welcome such an opportunity to be of service to the region.

A single parish or the council of churches may find a valuable ally in the local theater for focusing topics of concern to the whole community. Certainly the church cannot afford to pass up any chance to confront people with issues related to its life or the larger national or human welfare. Seldom will its tools or opportunities be more ecumenically focused than when it uses a secular medium and location for emphasizing, supporting, protesting, or discussing current issues. The theater and commercial film are for such purposes neutral ground.

In-Theater Viewing and Discussions Elsewhere

A second approach to use of the local theater as a focal point in a community forum is to hold discussions elsewhere after viewing the film in the theater. If a particular film is selected as a part of a larger community emphasis, all participating churches or agencies can recommend it to their constituents and suggest that they talk about it with other people or in a larger group. Emphasis should be on seeing the film sometime during the local run at the viewer's convenience. Participants might be provided in advance with a brief study guide or fact sheet about the film, with information as to where and when more or less formal efforts at discussion will take place. A section in the local paper could carry news of the issues or emphasis involved, or print a study guide, etc.

Places for discussion of the film by small groups are limitless. Restaurants, private homes, churches, even car pools and buses on the way to and from the theater suggest themselves. Local churches could open their lounges for discussion groups, serving coffee and a snack to any who would like to drop in after any showing of the film at the theater. Other information might be

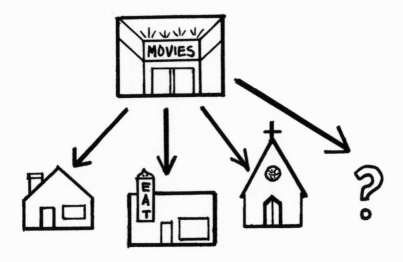

Individuals meet in groups in private homes, restaurants, churches, etc., following the film viewing in the theater.

provided there in terms of printed materials, books, etc., either to help in discussing the film or to give more background on the issues involved. Perhaps key people from the community could be available at certain churches after showings of the film, to serve as community resource persons on the subject at hand. Church members might act as discussion leaders after some brief instruction, where desired.

As to special programs during the run of the film, specific times can be set for those who have so far seen it and would like to become involved in a discussion opportunity as well as hearing others' comments on the film. The hall might be arranged with individual tables for small groups.

After opening remarks, the table groups can be put to work at discussing the picture and its issues, as suggested by the moderator for the evening or according to the groups themselves. After a half hour or so of table talk, the entire assembly might hear brief comments by a panel gathered from the smaller groups, or made

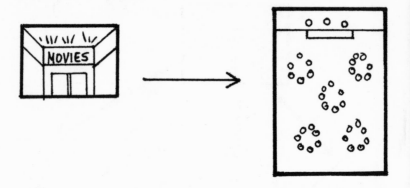

Theater film viewing and small groups meeting in a large hall in connection with a panel discussion of film.

up of persons having particular competence to deal with the film and its issues and invited beforehand for that purpose. When the panel had spoken, the audience would be invited to comment or raise questions.

The advantage of this approach would be to provide time for several kinds of experience: small groups, large groups, confronting the experts, etc. Also, more total time could be spent in depth discussions because the entire time of viewing the film would have taken place earlier.

A disadvantage of this general style of approach, focused in specific churches, halls, and so on, would be the tendency for each parish or organization to attract its own constituency, thus losing the more ecumenical possibilities for dialogue.

Local Theater Teamed with a Talk Radio Station

A more complicated but exciting framework for community dialogue centered in a secular film is the use of a radio talk-back station teamed with the theater and telephone. One such program took place in March 1969 in the Twin Cities of Minnesota, when the Warner Brothers–Seven Arts film *The Heart is a Lonely Hunter* came to the downtown Orpheum Theaters in Minneapolis and St. Paul, its first run in these cities. The program functioned at three levels.

The first was as a spontaneous experience in the normal sequence of events in the community. A special film trailer had been prepared announcing the talk-back opportunity over station WLOL. After the initial showing of the film on the evening of March 7, the trailer was flashed on the screen. (The cost of having it made was approximately $35.). It invited people to call in and discuss the film with the Program Host for the evening and a guest from the communication department of the University of Minnesota. In addition, the same information plus a brief study guide of the film was printed on a one-page flyer handed to theatergoers as they left after the show. There was no advance

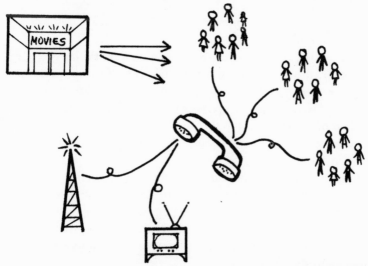

Theater film viewing with dialogue groups in homes and halls hooking up with radio and/or television talk-back shows where a panel is discussing the film.

publicity either by the theater, the newspapers, or the radio station. On the basis of a telephone busy-signal count and an analysis of the calls received by the station, it was learned that, while the total number of calls to the station did not increase that night, a third of those that got through concerned the film. Some were from people who had gone to the theater for entertainment and were responding to the invitation to call in with no other prompting. Other calls had been prompted by the comments of those who had seen the film at the theater. Thus a chain reaction kind of response was set in motion.

The second level operated on Sunday, March 9, involving specially prearranged viewing groups throughout the Twin Cities area. The makeup of the various groups was: youth (church), senior citizens, inner-city residents, suburban residents, college youth, and even one group of deaf persons. (The picture concerns two deaf-mutes.) These people attended the theater at the first afternoon showing and returned to homes, churches, and so on, where they spent approximately thirty to forty minutes discussing the film.

Neither the trailer nor the flyer circulated on Friday was used. However, more detailed study guides were distributed to each viewing group where they met. At an appointed time they tuned in to WLOL to listen to responses from other groups and phoned in their own comments. In this way they all shared in a community-wide, specific-subject dialogue which would have been impossible in any other way.

One of the significant finds, in evaluating this activity, was that the senior-citizen and other adult groups responded more favorably to the activity than did young people. This seems to indicate that such an approach can be helpful in involving the group of people which is often hardest to draw into educational opportunities in the community.

The third level of program took place on Tuesday, March 11. It operated in the same way as the first except that the activity was publicized by WLOL through spot announcements in order to involve as large a number of people as possible. The result of this

Would you like to talk about it?

You came to see The Heart Is a Lonely Hunter to be enter-
tained, but more than that has happened; something has happened in the area of your ideas and feelings. Questions
have been raised and answered. Feelings have been evoked.

Why not call WLOL and ask your question or state your
opinion.

698-5566 WLOL NIGHT LINE

For instance: What do you feel the film was all about?

> There were many tragedies in this film. Which
> one do you feel was the greatest tragedy?
>
> What is the view of man that this film pre-
> sents?
>
> What kinds of individual, personal needs were
> evident in the film? How were they met?
>
> Alienation is said to be the greatest problem
> of our time. Where did you see alienation in
> the film? What did the film say about possi-
> ble causes and cure?
>
> What comment did the film make on the kind of
> priorities in life that ought to govern ac-
> tions and aspirations?
>
> Which relationships determined how people be-
> haved? What might this say to parents?
>
> What do children have a right to expect of
> their parents?
>
> Do you think that the different relationship
> Mick had with her mother and her father is
> typical of the way it is in most families?
> Why?
>
> What was Mick really saying about her view of
> life when she said to Harry on the beach,
> "Please, let me have just one thing be the way
> I want it to be. Please."

promotion and the buildup of interest from previous levels of operation was that 83 percent of those phoning WLOL on Tuesday wanted to discuss the film, whereas on the previous Friday the situation was the inverse, with 33 percent of the callers discussing the film. There was thus a dramatic, cumulative momentum in community interest over the three segments in the five days of the program. Doubtless many regular listeners to the station took part in the discussion of issues in the film, though they had not seen it. This would indicate that the film as catalyst in such a community program makes an impact far beyond those immediately involved.

The program was regarded as highly successful by those who developed it. But one of the concomitant values was the effect on the theater and the radio station. According to the manager of the Orpheum Theatre, the film enjoyed a better box office than any film in the first three months of 1969, and for Tuesday evening showings that Tuesday's was the largest since the first of the year. While there may have been other factors unrelated to the film study program that increased the audience, it was felt by the management that the program had been of direct benefit. (Subsequent reports on the film revealed that in the Twin Cities it had the best box office in the country.)

There was also favorable reaction by the management of WLOL. Brad Johnson, Program Director of the station, said that the persistence of on-the-air discussion of issues after a program has ended is a clear barometer of its success. Especially on Sunday, the on-the-air discussion continued far into the night, and by this standard was eminently successful as a form of community dialogue.

The overall conclusion by those involved in the program, especially those who developed and promoted it,* was that the secular

*Mr. Eugene H. Bunge, Producer-Director, Channel 2, KTCA, St. Paul, Minnesota; Dr. Robert Clyde, Director Social Science Research Center of Augsburg College; Rev. Robert Konzelman, Director of Educational Research in Division of Parish Education of the American Lutheran Church.

motion picture and talk radio can be very successfully teamed as effective instruments for facilitating community discussion of significant issues.

There is evidence through other programs that local cable TV and educational TV channels can be similarly teamed with the local theater and telephone for community forums. In a masscom culture such options are becoming increasingly viable.

Special Screenings

In the early paragraphs of this chapter the effort of a community relations group in Minnetonka, Minnesota was described. Their approach in the use of secular film and the local theater as community forum centered on special screenings of a film as distinguished from current offerings in the theater.

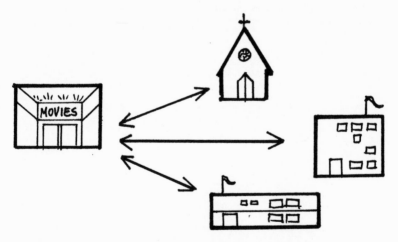

Special in-theater screening for schools and churches

Special screenings are possible in most communities, and can draw on older films, which may be selected for their relevance to local situations and not solely on the basis of current availability.

Use of films in this way may offer opportunity for longer preparation and promotion, since most managers do not know what pictures will be showing at their theaters much over a month or two ahead. Chapter 9 dealing with the Film Festival may be consulted for further insight into this mode of programming.

Use as Many Approaches as Possible

Depending on the scope of community involvement and the nature of the program being developed, variations of the approaches so far discussed may suggest themselves. However, for a community-wide dialogue centering on the local theater as a forum, effort should be made to use as many types of approach as possible to increase the impact and outreach. There can be little doubt that secular films viewed as relevant communication and serving as a catalytic agent for community dialogue offer exciting possibilities for parish youth and adult education regarding current social, political, moral, and religious issues.

11. FRIENDS WHO CAN HELP

There are certain basic facts about the motion picture industry in America which must be faced by anyone who hopes to use secular films in the service of the church. Recognizing them and guiding one's planning and action by them will save endless hours of fruitless effort and frustration.

The first fact to be recognized is that "the film industry" is technically a misnomer. This is a form of verbal shorthand used to refer broadly to the extremely complicated and numerous industries, crafts, skills, arts, trade unions, and guild organizations involved in the production, distribution, and exhibition of secular motion pictures in America. To lump together under the term "film industry" everything that has to do with secular films may therefore be a disservice to many. When someone is disgruntled over the kind of pictures being shown in the local theater, he is apt to condemn the "industry," when in fact on this occasion only the local theater manager is responsible; or an absentee landlord who presides over a vast real estate empire; or the chairman of the board of a financial institution in Boston; or some small independent film-maker with a used 16mm. camera. In other words, you cannot fairly pass out blame or praise for everything related to motion pictures in America to any one definite industry, person, or organization. Nor, by the same token, can you expect to find one person who is able by fiat to cut through all the red tape and business channels involved in exhibiting a film in a local theater on a certain date. Many intricate factors of economics, geography, politics, law, and social conscience must be worked through.

Second, it must be clearly understood that the film business is just that: a business, organized and operated for the purpose of making money. If it does not make a profit, it ceases to make motion pictures. This means that its decisions in regard to any phase of its operation are made, not on the basis of educational, religious, or otherwise benevolent principles or ideals, but quite simply for and by financial considerations. If it can be involved in, or in any way contribute to, educational, religious, or benevolent programs and still make money it usually will, but these are secondary.

If you are to use secular films in the service of the church, therefore, you must not expect to do so at the expense or loss of the "film industry," or by a gesture of pure philanthropy on its part. Your film program must provide the industry with income commensurate with the service rendered. Thus if you can devise programs that bring no financial loss to the theater—or even produce increased income—you will get far better cooperation than if you expect the theater to be the church's benefactor. A local manager who cooperates with you in an educational program may wish to extend certain advantages, courtesies, or gifts in gratitude for any increase in business he receives through your activities; but if he does so, it is his privilege and not the church's right.

In calling attention to the commercial aspects of the film industry, I do not intend to disparage or discredit anyone involved in it. The purpose here is simply to indicate clearly that since secular films are a commodity for sale, the principles that govern their production and use are not different from those that govern General Motors, Westinghouse, Sears Roebuck, or the local gas and electric companies. We expect to pay for the products or service provided by any one of them.

On the other side of the ledger, it must be acknowledged that even if we pay through ticket purchases at the box office the going rate for the use of product and facilities offered, we get a tremendous bargain. The church could not possibly afford to produce such costly tools and facilities for its educational program.

Before moving on, I want to say that many of the people you will encounter at all levels of the "industry," from local theater managers to chief executive officers of major companies, are, like the rest of us, fathers or mothers, community residents and members of churches, who are genuinely concerned for the total welfare of the community and the nation, and will do everything possible to cooperate in an effort in the interest of community welfare.

Third, and closely related to the foregoing, is the fact that not everyone in the film industry is a specialist in the meaning, making, or use of films. This very large and varied business enterprise seeks at each level of its operation the most competent people it can afford for the specific tasks that need to be done. Because films are mass-produced and marketed, much of the work involved requires no more knowledge of them as an art form, educational tool, or cultural force than a person in any other occupation might have. The advertising executive for a film company uses the same skills called for and used by the corresponding executive of a soap company or automobile manufacturer. In many cases the manager of a local theater needs little more knowledge of film to do his job than would the manager of an apartment house; the primary task of each is to rent space—one in the shape and size of living quarters, the other in the form of seats for short-term occupancy. The manager of one might very well adapt his skills to the other. Because people work in some phase of the film industry does not necessarily mean that they understand or appreciate what the church is trying to do in using secular films in educational contexts.

This means that in working with a local theater manager and others in developing a film study opportunity or program, you as pastor or educator may have to take the initiative in the selection of films and planning their use, even to suggesting ways in which the theater can assist with the physical arrangements for the program. It may be that you will need to spend some time helping the manager to understand better the nature and educational potential of motion pictures. After all, he is paid to manage real estate, not to be an educator. But you and he together have insights and resources that may be of great mutual benefit, rendering a larger service to the church, the motion picture industry, and the community than either could alone.

A Quick Shot of Industry Structures

At the risk of oversimplification, I should like to describe the film industry in America in terms of its three basic functions: production, distribution, and exhibition, illustrated in the diagram on p. 109.

Of these three levels of operation, anyone trying to use secular films for educational purposes in a local situation will probably have most direct contact with the film exhibitor. But some knowledge of the other levels will prove useful in understanding why the exhibitor can or cannot do certain things.

Film Production

The level of film production is perhaps the most dramatic and mysterious of the three. There the image-makers and the glamorous folk we read about—directors, actors, and actresses—are at work. Though these few individuals occupy the limelight, they are surrounded and supported by thousands of unseen people who man the hardware and do the technical jobs necessary to film-making. Here the production companies, large and small, are at work planning production schedules, buying or renting properties, building sets and organizing for specific projects. It

Functional Chart of the Motion Picture Industry in America

Major Functions	Agencies and Tasks		Relation to General Public
FILM PRODUCTION (Product design and development)	Individuals—Independent Companies—Large Corporations (Writers, directors, actors, tradesmen, craftsmen etc.) (Motion Picture Association of America)		Magazine and news coverage (Product and people) Image-building
FILM DISTRIBUTION (Merchandising—display and sales)	National Advertising and Public Relations Offices Regional Offices for Promotion and Sales SCREENINGS BOOKINGS *for* →		
FILM EXHIBITION (Real estate management)	Regional Offices of Theater Management Companies Local Offices for Management—Owners—Managers—Bookers Local Theater Booking and Exhibition of Films (Property management, etc.) (National Association of Theater Owners)		Local theaters Newspaper ads TV and radio advertising, etc. Community relations

is at this level that the decisions are made as to what the product to be screened in the 14,000 local theaters shall be.

While Hollywood is regarded as the film capital, actual filming is often done at remote locations throughout the world, frequently in the small towns of America, while many of the major film companies are actually managed from offices in New York City. Large corporations, such as those belonging to the Motion Picture Association of America, and smaller independent companies formed for the production of single specific films share common concerns and do essentially the same kinds of things. But behind them all, small or large, are the financiers who invest the money that makes all the other activities possible. In the final analysis, those who supply the money make the ultimate decisions as to the character and content of secular films.

It is at this level that arrangements are made to send the motion pictures across the land to area or regional film exchanges manned by representatives of the major film companies and conglomerates. From these centers (at the second level), the films are threaded into the network of theaters in cities and towns and thus woven into the fabric of America's local community life.

Though there are, by comparison to the "greats," many small film production companies, their product is usually channeled through one of the larger organizations for release and distribution. The major companies of the film industry are at present:

> American International
> Avco Embassy
> Buena Vista/Walt Disney
> Cinerama
> Columbia Pictures Corporation
> Metro-Goldwyn-Mayer, Incorporated
> National General
> Paramount Pictures Corporation
> Twentieth Century Fox Films

United Artists Corporation
Universal Pictures
Warner Brothers-Seven Arts, Inc.

Each of these companies is involved not only in production, but also in the distribution of its product. They have regional offices in major cities across the country from which they carry on negotiations with exhibitors to get the films shown. These distributors have no control over the local theater except through the pricing of their product, which may in some cases determine whether or not a local theater can book the film.

At the national level the advertising and promotion program for each film is designed, even to the format of newspaper ads for use in local communities, and established with precise requirements as to the comparative size and relationship of type and type faces used to designate the names of stars, supporting actors and actresses, authors, director, producer, and so on. Strategies for releasing a particular film are meticulously worked out to take maximum advantage of times, seasons, geography, word-of-mouth report, current events, etc. All these have a bearing upon the *how* and *when* and *how long* of the church's ability to make use of a specific film.

An interesting example of the way in which current events determine the release and exhibition strategy for a picture may be seen in the handling of the Frankovich-Sturges production, *Marooned.* This film was scheduled to open in many cities the very week that Apollo Thirteen was in danger of being marooned in space. Consequently the film was withheld from exhibition until the national shock and fear for the safety of the Apollo team had abated.

The many stories in national magazines and newspapers, or on television and radio, about persons in the film industry are not accidental. They are carefully planned and planted so as to provide a backdrop of public interest or curiosity for forthcoming films.

BILLING

Warner Bros.-Seven Arts 25%
  presents

ALAN ARKIN 100%
  in

"THE HEART IS A LONELY HUNTER" 100%
  Co-Starring

LAURINDA BARRETT

STACY KEACH, JR.

CHUCK McCANN   } No percentage

BIFF McGUIRE   } All same size

PERCY RODRIGUEZ   } Alphabetical order

CICELY TYSON
  And Introducing

SONDRA LOCKE 50%

Technicolor® 15%

  From the novel by
CARSON McCULLERS 15%

  Screenplay by
THOMAS C. RYAN 15%

  Music by
DAVE GRUSIN 5%

  Executive Producer
JOEL FREEMAN 15%

  Produced by
THOMAS C. RYAN and MARC MERSON 15%

  Directed by
ROBERT ELLIS MILLER 15%

Comparative values of print size and type required for use in advertising copy for a film. Such matters are determined by advertising departments of the film company, not the local manager.

All this has interesting implications for those who seek to use secular films in the service of the church. Since the public media (press, radio, and TV), through feature articles, news comments, reviews, etc., are creating interest in forthcoming pictures, the effect is to provide the church with an early warning system for films. Clues to potentially useful films are there, but what is more, a climate of interest and acceptance among the church constituency is also being built up, which can be very useful when directed to the church's purposes in film utilization.

Another kind of impact on the local community emanating from the film production level is the work of the Motion Picture Association of America. This is a voluntary organization of the major film companies I have listed. It has its roots in the Motion Picture Producers and Distributors of America, Inc., established in 1922 under the leadership of Will Hays, a member of President Harding's Cabinet.

The goals and purposes of the organization have remained virtually the same, namely, to foster the common interests of the member companies in relation to the federal government and the general public. Jack Valenti, President of the MPAA since 1968, like Will Hays, the organization's first executive, was a member of the staff of a President of the United States (he served in the White House under President Johnson). This, I think, is a measure of both the prestige and the importance of the MPAA in the eyes of its constituency. With headquarters at 522 Fifth Avenue, New York City, it operates offices also in Washington, D.C. and Hollywood.

It is through the MPAA that the film industry seeks to regulate itself in terms of moral and artistic standards, advertising, and film titles. The Production Code, the Advertising Code, and a Title Registration Bureau are its main agencies for internal control. Their obvious purpose is to forestall the necessity of public or legal consorship. The latest effort toward self-regulation has been the film rating system mentioned in Chapter 2.

Member organizations are represented in the fields of law,

research, and public relations by the association. A major effort toward film understanding, selection, and utilization is made through the Community Services Department, headed for many years by Mrs. Margaret Twyman. Through this office, film societies are promoted and other efforts made to inform parents, teachers, and the general public of the educational and artistic values of certain secular films. Materials related to these emphases may be obtained by writing to the Community Services Department of the New York office.

At the level of the local community, direct contact with persons and agencies for production and distribution of motion pictures is practically nil. Nonetheless, the local parish or community has a highly influential voice in this remote, mysterious world of film production. It is transmitted to the decision-makers through the whirr and ring of the cash registers in the box offices of the 14,000 local theaters. From these come the votes for whatever kind of film fare America is going to have. And more importantly, it is the only vote that has any power to affect either the moral or the artistic quality of motion pictures. Thus, totally apart from the educational advantages and values of using secular films in programs of religious education, there is the need to support the production of quality films in the public interest.

Film Distribution

At the distribution level most of the work is directed to business relationships with the exhibitors. Through representatives of the film companies, screenings of the latest film product are held for exhibitors, local film critics, and others for whom a particular film may have special interest. Sometimes special screenings are held for ministers and other educators. The goal of such screenings is always to provide a setting in which favorable word-of-mouth promotion can be generated for the film. The whole thrust of the

distribution system is to "sell" (rent) the films for local exhibition.

It is at this level of the industry that the producer must obtain
his financial return to cover the costs of production and make a
profit for the investors. The distributor therefore enters into
contracts with exhibitors for play dates and sums to be paid for
the privilege. Once a contract is signed, the local theater is obli-
gated to show the film on the agreed dates. The exhibitor cannot
withdraw the film and substitute another without renegotiating
the contract. In many cases the distributor requires a guaranteed
amount plus a percentage of the income. However, most often
the distributor receives a flat percentage of the gross revenue
from showing a film.

Each contract is individually tailored to the local situation. No
two theaters need pay the same amount for a film rental, since
their individual potentials and past records are different. The
same situation prevails in regard to marketing areas or geograph-
ical locations. Each area has a different history and potential. A
theater in Columbus, Ohio, playing the same film as a theater in
downtown New York City, will not necessarily pay the same price
for the privilege.

In some areas films cannot be shown until they have played in
other locations. For instance, a picture may not be available for
DuBuque, Iowa until it has played in Des Moines, or for St.
Cloud, Minnesota before it has played in Minneapolis. Even
within a metropolitan area there are priorities. A film may not be
sold to a theater in suburban Oak Park, Illinois, before it has
played downtown Chicago.

All this relates to the master strategy determined for a particular film at the national level of distribution. Some pictures are
released directly to local neighborhood theaters without ever
running downtown, while others are limited to playing only
downtown houses for long periods of time.

The task of the film distributor is that of weaving a picture into

the fabric of community life in the most economically profitable
way for the film company. In relation to the national strategy for
the release, he will carefully modulate where and when a film may
be shown and at what price. In some cases it may be profitable
to permit it to be played in a certain community in disregard of
the normal pattern, while at other times this would be disastrous.

What this means is that anyone desiring to use secular films in
a religious education program is limited by many factors which
must be carefully explored before definite plans can be formu-
lated. In Chapter 10 I described a situation in which it was possible and advantageous for the film company, the local theater, and
the church to alter their normal procedures. It is not always so
easy. Two illustrations on the negative side will demonstrate this.

In October 1970 the American Lutheran Church was to hold
its biennial convention in San Antonio, Texas. At this convention
certain issues and policy matters related to family life, social
service agencies, and educational strategies were to be decided.
At that very time, Columbia Pictures was releasing *I Never Sang
for My Father.* Prior to its release, the author had prepared a study
guide for the film as a part of the Dialogue Thrust in Films
program of the denomination's Division of Parish Education. It
was thought that the screening of this particular film for the
convention would be extremely advantageous, providing a national spotlight on the picture for the film company and constitut-
ing a very valuable educational experience for the delegates
related to convention issues.

An approach was made to the New York office of Columbia
Pictures, which went to work to make the project possible. But
even at that level it was impossible to work out an arrangement
so the film could be screened in a downtown San Antonio theater
during the convention. The desired theaters were under contract
on the convention dates to exhibit the pictures of another film
company. Thus, in order to screen *I Never Sang for My Father* at
the desired place and time, it would have been necessary for the
church or Columbia Pictures to pay several thousand dollars to

the other company for the privilege of interrupting its contract. Neither party felt that the educational experience and publicity which might accrue from and for the film was worth that kind of investment. So the project had to be dropped.

Another illustration of how business contracts can limit possibilities took place in Gettysburg, Pennsylvania in the spring of 1971. Students in a course on the use of mass media, in cooperation with churches of various denominations in the community, planned a community Film Study Festival for the four Tuesday nights following Easter. The films selected to be shown on those dates were: *Cromwell, I Never Sang for My Father, The Heart Is a Lonely Hunter,* and *The Learning Tree.* The first two (Columbia Pictures) were currently in release but not yet scheduled for Gettysburg. The latter two (Warner Brothers–Seven Arts) were 1968 and 1969 releases. Early in January, contacts with the manager of the local Majestic Theater were begun and details worked out over the next two and a half months. The program was cleared with the regional management of the company owning the theater. But two weeks before the first film was to be shown, the sponsoring student and church group was notified that, unknown to either the local or the regional manager, the theater had been placed under contract for other films on the nights of the festival. The result was the cancellation of the festival. Again, everyone was for the idea, but agreements could not be set aside.

Though several factors had intervened to complicate the process at Gettysburg, and the group was encouraged to try the project again in the fall, the lesson is clear. Plans for such programs must begin very early and must be negotiated with those who really have authority to make decisions, both as to the availability of a film and of the local theater in which it is to be played. In this particular situation, the obstacle was located at the distribution level in agreements between the theater management company and the film distributor.

I shall return to this situation with additional information in the next section. Suffice it to say that, since the normal pattern of operation places the film distributor in contact with the exhibitor, persons trying to arrange an educational use of films will not generally come in touch with those working at the distribution level. Contacts with them usually take place through the local exhibitor.

Film Exhibition

Though the film exhibition phase of the motion picture industry is most conspicuous in a given community, it is nonetheless the furthest removed from "showbiz." At the exhibition level, the film business becomes in reality a real estate business. The local theater, whether owned privately or by a chain or management company, represents a property investment, the return for which comes from "renting" individual seats for limited periods of time. The film shown is the means of encouraging people to rent a seat. Though this may be an oversimplification, it will help to view the matter so.

There was a time when the people who actually produced motion pictures also owned the local theaters. Reminders of it are still evident in the marquee names of many of the older theaters. (Paramount, Fox, United Artists, etc.). However, anti-trust laws were brought to bear on this situation in 1947, and the Supreme Court ruled against the ownership of theater circuits by motion picture producers. Very often, therefore, people who know or care little about film as art or as an educational force are those with whom you will be working in using secular films in local theaters.

In smaller communities theaters are sometimes owned by individuals. Most, however, are the property of management companies called circuits. These range from small local organizations with several theaters in a single city up through those like Mid-continent Theaters of Minneapolis, which owns theaters in three different states, to giants such as General Cinema Corporation, Loew's Corporation, N.G.C. Corporation, and United Artists Theater Circuit, Inc., which have many theaters in many states. There are approximately 700 circuits in the United States having four or more houses. These operate 53 percent of the total number of theaters in this country. If a theater is privately owned and operated, the owner-operator relates directly to the distributor for the film company, booking whatever films he can obtain or desires to exhibit in his community.

Houses owned by a management company are operated by local resident managers whose major responsibility lies in seeing that the physical premises are maintained; hiring and paying projectionists, ushers, ticket and popcorn sellers, and janitors; placing newspaper ads and/or spot announcements on radio and TV; and seeing that films scheduled for showing through the regional offices of the management company are screened and sent on their way again. Some resident managers are interested in films for their own sake and can be very helpful. Others are simply interested in the business aspects of their job.

Usually the management company will have one or more regional offices and will employ bookers. Their task is to attend film screenings and be aware of forthcoming products, and to understand the kinds of films which will receive the best acceptance in each community where theaters are operated. In such operations, resident managers of local theaters may simply be told what films are booked for what dates. But where the manager is alert and sensitive, he will endeavor to indicate to the company's booker what films may be most desirable in his community at any time.

This means that, while the whole process of film exhibition may be quite mechanical and irresponsible, it can also be very responsible and creative. Those who seek to use secular films in the service of the church's educational ministry should become familiar with how the local theater is operated and how interested in and informed about film the manager really is. Where there is informed, alert management, pastors and educators will be able to carry on their film negotiations with that one person. Where the resident manager is of another temperament, it may be necessary to deal directly with regional managers or bookers. Who these people are can be learned through the local theater manager. But in any case it is important that congenial relations with resident managers be maintained.

In many instances the very fact that community leaders are taking an interest in the local theater may be a means of encouragement to an otherwise disinterested and joyless functionary of a large corporation, who sees no meaning in what he does except that it provides him with a regular paycheck. Creative cooperation with local theater management may contribute much to the moral, religious, educational, and cultural climate of a community.

In these pages I have tried to indicate some of the things that must be known about the film industry if effective use of secular films is to be achieved. While much more might be said, most of it can also be learned by direct involvement. This small volume may help to avoid certain frustrating and defeating roadblocks, and to some extent encourage the reader to discover his own way through a very complicated set of circumstances.

In conclusion, it must be recognized that if the people I have been talking about in this chapter were aware of the potential of their product for religious and educational use, these pages would be unnecessary. They would have done it all for us long ago. It is your task, therefore, as pastor/educator to explore the possibilities with them. You may be their teacher and benefactor, just as they may be yours.

Bibliography

The books here listed give a more detailed development of the basic ideas in the present volume. It is a beginning—not a complete list. Fuller bibliographies may be found in most of the books here named, and through them the reader may follow his own particular interests.

Arnheim, Rudolf. *Toward a Psychology of Art.* Berkeley, Calif.: University of California Press, 1967. Insights into the psychology of film viewing.

Babin, Pierre, ed. *The Audio Visual Man.* Dayton, Ohio: George A. Pflaum, 1970. Essays on various aspects of media use in our visually oriented culture.

Barnouw, Eric. *Mass Communication: Television, Radio, Film, Press.* New York: Holt, Rinehart & Winston, 1956. Classic analysis of the psychology, history, media, and sponsors of mass communications.

Carpenter, Edmund, and McLuhan, Marshall, eds. *Explorations in Communication.* Boston: Beacon Press (P), 1960. The nature and meaning of contemporary communications.

* Eisenstein, Sergei. *Film Form and Film Sense.* New York: Meridian Press (P), 1965.

Everson, William K. *The American Movie.* New York: Atheneum, 1963. Survey of film history.

Feyen, Sharon, ed. *Screen Experience: An Approach to Film.* Dayton, Ohio: George A. Pflaum, 1969. Guide to setting up a variety of film programs, with basic introductions to film and its language.

*Classic books on film, important in film education. (P) Paperback.

Fischer, Edward. *The Screen Arts.* New York: Sheed & Ward, 1960. Some norms for film and television appreciation and criticism.

Fore, William F. *Image and Impact: How Man Comes Through in the Mass Media.* New York: Friendship Press, 1970. Brief but perceptive comment on the cultural impact of mass media.

Gattegno, Caleb. *Toward a Visual Culture.* New York: Outerbridge and Dienstfrey, 1969. Provocative discussion of the educational value of sight over language.

Houston, Penelope. *The Contemporary Cinema.* Baltimore: Penguin Books (P), 1963. Survey of the international postwar cinema and analysis of the motion picture industry.

Hurley, Neil P. *Theology Through Film.* New York: Harper & Row, 1970. A cinematic theology illustrated by reference to major films.

Huss, Roy, and Silverstein, Norman. *Film Experience.* New York: Dell Publishing Co., Delta Book, 1969. Good basic introduction to film language.

Jones, G. Williams. *Sunday Night at the Movies.* Richmond, Va.: John Knox Press (P), 1968. The why and how of church involvement in film interpretation and criticism. Guide for planning and executing a film discussion program.

Kahle, Roger, and Lee, Robert E. A. *Popcorn and Parables.* Minneapolis: Augsburg Publishing House, 1971. Brief general discussion of films in the United States, their effect and use in our culture.

Klapper, Joseph T. *The Effects of Mass Communications.* New York: Free Press, 1960. Pre-McLuhan review of research on the effects of mass communications on people.

*Knight, Arthur. *The Liveliest Art.* New York: New American Library (P), 1957. Film history in the 1950s.

*Kracauer, Siegfried. *From Caligari to Hitler: A Psychological History of the German Film.* Princeton, N.J.: Princeton University Press (P), 1947. Authoritative history of German film.

Kuhns, William. *The Electronic Gospel.* New York: Herder & Herder, 1969. Deals with the media environment and compares the religious and entertainment milieus in terms of meaning.

————. *Environmental Man.* New York: Harper & Row, 1969. Deals with the effects of changing environment on man's beliefs and relationships.

Lynch, William E., S.J. *Image Industries: A Constructive Analysis of Films and Television.* London: Sheed & Ward, 1959. Evaluates and criticizes the image-making of the television and film industries.

MacCann, Richard Dyer. *Film and Society.* New York: Charles Scribner's Sons (P), 1964. The effect and influence of movies on society.

_____. *Film: A Montage of Theories.* New York: E. P. Dutton & Co. (P), 1966. Probably the best available single book on film theory.

McAnany, Emil, and Williams, Robert. *The Film Viewer's Handbook* Glen Rock, N.J.: Paulist Press (P), 1965. Suggestions for film programs. Discussion guides for several films.

McLuhan, Marshall. *The Mechanical Bride: Folklore of Industrial Man.* Boston: Beacon Press (P), 1951. Earliest of McLuhan's books. Cultural significance of comic strips, gangster magazines, popular ads.

_____. *The Gutenberg Galaxy.* Toronto: University of Toronto Press (P), 1962. McLuhan thesis on effect of the printing press on man's perception.

_____. *Understanding Media: The Extensions of Man.* New York: McGraw-Hill Book Co. (P), 1964. Attempts to explore the electronic media revolution.

_____. *The Medium Is the Massage.* New York: Bantam Books (P), 1967. Brief introduction to McLuhan's thought.

Mendelsohn, Harold. *Mass Entertainment.* New Haven: College and University Press, 1966. Discusses in a scholarly way the effect and function of mass entertainment in our culture.

Powdermaker, Hortense. *Hollywood: The Dream Factory.* New York: Grosset & Dunlap (P), 1950. Anthropological study of Hollywood's people and beliefs.

Steinberg, Charles, ed. *Mass Media and Communication.* New York: Hastings House, 1966. The impact and significance of the communication arts in a mass society.

Wall, James M. *A Way of Viewing Film.* Grand Rapids, Mich.: Wm B. Eerdmans Publishing Co., 1971. Presents a way of critically evaluating film.

72 73 74 75 10 9 8 7 6 5 4 3 2 1